INTERTWINED

INTERTWINED

The Art of Handspun Yarn, Modern Patterns, and Creative Spinning

BEVERLY MASSACHUSETTS

QUARRY BOOKS

LEXI BOEGER

First published in the United States of America by
Quarry Books, a member of
Quayside Publishing Group
100 Cummings Center
Suite 406-L
Beverly, Massachusetts 01915-6101
Telephone: (978) 282-9590
Fax: (978) 283-2742
www.quarrybooks.com

Library of Congress Cataloging-in-Publication Data
Boeger, Lexi.
  Intertwined : creativity, collaboration, and the art of handspun yarn / Lexi Boeger.
    p. cm.
  ISBN 1-59253-374-4
  1. Hand spinning. 2. Spun yarns. I. Title.
  TT847.B655 2008
  746.1'2--dc22

                                    2007024808

ISBN-13: 978-1-59253-374-9
ISBN-10: 1-59253-374-4

10 9 8 7 6 5 4 3 2

Cover Design: 12 E Design
Book Design: Dawn DeVries Sokol
Cover Image: Lexi Boeser
Illustrations: "At a Glance" illustrations by Lexi Boeger
Tech Editor: Jean Lampe
Photography: All photography by Lexi Boeger, unless otherwise noted
Printed in China

To the Reverend Dr. Joel "nano" Warner

CONTENTS

A Balanced Yarn

Handspun yarn is more than simply yarn. It is a creative endeavor. It has an intrinsic integrity that is built into the yarn by the very act of spinning. Every inch has been fed through the hand of the craftsperson. Formed. Changed. Created. Thought-through. Felt.

Handspun yarns are made by conscious beings, not unconscious machines. This imbues them with an internal energy, giving them character and uniqueness. Each yarn is a reflection of the individual spinner who made it. It is this quality that makes handspun yarn so amazing to work with. As you work through a skein, you can see, inch by inch, the decisions that the spinner made. It passes before you just like a story.

Though a spinner's individuality is reflected in a yarn, the process the yarn goes through reaches beyond the individual spinner. The spinner is just one stop on a journey, one in which the yarn is perpetually destined for new hands. When you wrap yourself in a scarf made with handspun yarn, you can trace each stitch the knitter made. This connects you to the knitter through his or her work, just as the knitter is connected to the spinner through theirs. The yarn passed through the knitter's fingers just as it passed through the hand of the spinner; the fiber passed through the hand of the spinner just as it passed through the hand of the person who dyed it, and so on through the hand of the farmer who raised the animal, sheared it, and washed it. This phenomenon joins together hands through a single strand that stretches across spaces and through time. The yarn becomes a bond that connects separate people into a collaborative group, all working toward a common creation. The final form that the yarn takes is not the work of one artisan, but the synthesis of many.

A balanced yarn is one that beams with individuality yet is a record of this collective history. A spinner achieves balance if they can be proud of their creativity while being comfortable sharing the credit. This is a way of thinking that can be applied beyond the craft of spinning. Each piece of a puzzle needs to be unique, yet each piece must lend itself to the whole to make it work. This is the balance.

Traditionally spun yarn by Lou Andersen, Lofty Lou's, Placerville, California; nontraditional yarn by Laurence Pocztar (France) of LaineZinZin

The Art of Craft

The dramatic changes in how yarns are spun is creating some shifts and rifts within the handspinning community, and as a result, the craft of handspinning is experiencing some growing pains. The conventional view of spinning is that a yarn must function as a component to a final material or garment. Its value lies in how well it fulfills this role. Qualities such as balance, strength, and consistency are regarded as the hallmarks of good spinning. Traditional spinning does not diverge far from its roots, using tried and true fibers such as wool, cotton, and silk. Spinning has reflected a close tie to its historic past and a satisfaction in maintaining these historic methods and materials.

But things are changing. There is an explosion of new materials being spun, expanding the definition of what constitutes yarn. New techniques that break all the traditional rules of spinning are changing the definition of how yarn is made. Yarn has become a medium for personal, social, and creative expression.

This shift happens in all craft genres, as the tension between the traditional roots and function of a craft and the human drive for creativity and fulfillment of our deeper intellectual and creative needs diverge. This tension often creates a rift between the proponents on either side, and the craft becomes divided into opposing groups. Sometimes these groups even become alienated from each other. The traditional group may view the diverging group as illegitimate newcomers, while the new group sees the traditional craftspeople as short-sighted and obsolete. Such a black-and-white view of the situation is not necessary, however. Not only is it a negative way to operate, but it also robs both groups of the opportunity to learn from each other. Both sides are valid, and both views are necessary for a craft to be relevant and balanced.

Striking a balance between tradition and innovation is imperative for keeping spinning from becoming a forgotten art. A craft is only truly viable if it resonates within the culture. Make it applicable to the times, and it will grow and change with the times. Arts are lost when a culture can't relate to them, either because technology makes the skill obsolete or because there is no longer a need for the product. This happened to handspun yarn as a result of two inventions: in 1764, James Hargreaves invented his famous multi-spool spinning wheel, called the Spinning Jenny. This was followed in the early eighteenth century with the invention of wool and cotton mills. The advent of commercial machinery that could produce consistent, strong, balanced yarns quickly and cheaply took handspinning out of society's necessary repertoire of skills. Only a small number of people continued to practice the art, and the skill has become a novelty, moving from the socioeconomic stage to the personal realm. It is enriching for the few who pursue it, but it no longer has much influence in our popular culture.

Adapting to the aesthetics of current popular culture will actually preserve traditional spinning as it opens the craft up to new advancements. Getting a larger number of people interested in handspun yarn will ensure that the craft is *not lost*. There are all types of knitters. Some will embrace the new innovative styles while others will prefer the traditional forms.

The Function of Creativity

Hopefully, most people will learn to appreciate *both* traditional spinning and its contemporary innovations for their different but equally valuable qualities. Skill and functionality are the building blocks of good spinning. Every spinner should be able to spin perfectly balanced, sound yarn *first*. This is the only way to gain a full understanding of the mechanics of yarn making and how the fibers behave. You have to know the rules before you can break them. There is an inverse relationship between control and creativity. It's like realism and abstraction. Say you are painting a leaf. The more realistically you try to paint it, the more abstract it becomes. The closer you observe the subject and try to replicate its every detail, the more your rendition dissolves into blurs, shapes, and colors. It is the scrutinizing, close observation of the reality that discloses the extreme abstraction of the painting.

The same thing happens when trying to spin perfect yarn. No matter how even the yarn or how smooth the roving, there is inevitably a little lump, a fiber out of place. You realize that perfection cannot be attained, that it is forever a receding horizon. The pursuit of perfection spotlights the incidences of imperfection.

The investigation of imperfection leads to creativity. A route to creativity is found through the attempt to master the skill. You can focus so closely on perfect mastery that you go through the eye of a needle and you come out the other side into a creative world thrown wide open.

If skill and function are the core of spinning, then creativity should envelop it, like a good core-spun yarn with strength on the inside and something beautiful or interesting on the outside. A drive for functionality is part of our inherent human nature, but so is the need for creativity. It is necessary for intellectual engagement, visual stimulation, and emotional fulfillment. From the very first moment that our ancestors put paint on their wall or a string of beads on their neck we have been creative, just as we have been functional from the first rock chiseled into a tool. These are the conditions that make us human, and we need to have both to be balanced. And so should good handspun yarn. It should be an equal reflection of both craftsmanship and idea.

Anemone, thick-and-thin single in wool and mohair with wire, metallic thread, and jelly-cord pompoms

Right: Sea life from the California coast, or the source of inspiration for the yarn, *Anemone*

chapter 1

Inspiration:
INTERNAL AND EXTERNAL RESOURCES FOR CREATIVITY

Creative spinning is a process of recognizing what inspires you and then breaking that down into elements that fit within the constructs of a yarn. It's a matter of identifying a subject and then asking yourself, "How do I translate that into spun fiber?" The boundaries of a yarn are simple and few. It needs to be spun and it needs to be continuous. But the possibilities for subject matter, style, texture, and meaning are infinite.

Sources of inspiration are also infinite. Ideas for color schemes, design concepts, textures, uses, and more can be gleaned from all areas of our world … the natural and urban landscape, weather, wildlife, manmade materials, products, and even refuse. We can be moved by the shifts and tides that undulate through our culture as well as our own internal perspective, feelings, and experience. Learning to extract what is rich, interesting, and meaningful from your world and from yourself, and channeling that into your spinning, will make your yarns creative and engaging.

External Inspiration

Landscape and the Natural World

The natural environment is a never-ending inspirational resource for color, movement, and textural possibilities. Next time a view or scene grabs your attention, don't just think, "Wow ... what a pretty spot." Ask yourself what it is about that view or place that is speaking to you. Is it the combination of colors? The atmospheric qualities? The movement of the leaves or grass? Identify just what it is that's compelling about the scene, then think about how to translate that into your yarn.

Capturing the essence of what you are seeing may seem difficult, and you might be tempted to take a photograph so you can refer to it later. Do not do this. First, every camera is different and will produce its own version of the subject. The colors may be different and the scene will not have the same feeling on a print as it did in the moment you experienced it. Rather, leave it to your memory. Stand there, observe it, soak it in, shut your eyes, and picture it. Memory is an interesting thing. It is not a dry recording of facts; rather, it

Woodland, two-yarn set of extra-coily two-ply hand-dyed merino paired with a bulky hand-dyed Icelandic wool single in Redwood Brown Sparkle.

Above: Redwood grove and pond: color inspiration for *Woodland* yarn

is an infusion of imagery, sensory experience, perspective, and emotion. These are exactly the qualities you want to preserve when recalling what you saw. So what if the green in your memory is brighter than it really was? Amplified in your memory are the things that compelled you. So, amplify them in your work.

Color

Mother Nature puts colors together in ways we would never think of. She dares to wear chartreuse with hot pink and chocolate brown. No, it's not a fashion nightmare—it's refreshing and interesting. Use five different shades of green, all in one yarn? Why not? If you love the mixtures of green found in the meadow, you'll love it on your head. Recreating the colors at home is simple enough. It does not matter what brand of dyes you use or whether they are natural or chemical—the trick to great color is to blend, blend, *blend*! Mother Nature rarely uses primary colors or the standards put out by dye manufacturers.

tip: When blending colors, don't throw all your fiber in before you test it. Follow the directions on your dyes to prepare the dye bath, then mix your colors approximately. Take a small piece of fiber and dip it in. If the color is not right, add a little more of this or that color, then dip another bit of fiber in. Keep dipping and tweaking until you get just the color you are looking for.

tip: Want to make brown on purpose? Mix any two colors that are directly opposite each other on the color wheel, such as red and green or blue and orange.

Texture

The importance of texture in creating a compelling yarn cannot be stressed enough. Watch people walk through a clothing store or yarn store and observe what they do. They touch. It's a gentle, unconscious action, but one that is

continues on page 16

Strangeland, hand-dyed, hand-carded wool with jute thread "tumbleweeds."

Above: Dunes and brush, an example from the natural landscape of the juxtaposition of smooth and scratchy, recreated in *Strangeland* yarn

essential to our assessment of a fiber, yarn, or material. The natural world is a cornucopia of textures, all of which can potentially be recreated in your yarns. It is a matter of matching a spinable fiber to the texture you want to recreate.

Replicating waves of grass? Leave the unspun ends of hemp, linen, or other plant-fiber roving sticking out of the yarn. Want lumpy dirt? Use uncarded natural brown, short-fibered wool spun extra chunky. Once you begin to look at your surroundings in terms of fiber, and your fiber in terms of your surroundings, the possibilities for creative spinning will grow exponentially.

Movement

The motion that pulses through our surroundings is not often consciously appreciated, but the effect it has on our perceptions is substantial. A field of wheat may be pretty, but a field of wheat in a gentle breeze can be mesmerizing. The same holds true for your yarn, especially if you are going to wear it. So, consider the way things move in nature and integrate that into the concept for your yarn. If a slow-moving fog bank is alluring then consider the qualities your yarn must have to emulate that effect. It must be light, airy, lofty, and translucent. Silver clouds of mohair spun extra loose and lofty on a sparkly thread core should do the trick!

Culture

Popular (and unpopular) culture is a rich source of inspiration for creative yarn making, from fashion and music to holidays and current events. Our culture is a living and changing entity to which we are each inextricably connected. Our individual relationship to the culture is like breathing; we take it in and it influences us, then we react and create, influencing it in return. The culture provides creative fodder for everything from simple design decisions to complex conceptual ideas.

Color

For color ideas, look to trends in fashion and design. Thumb through a current fashion magazine and look for nothing but color, for example. Squint your eyes to blur your vision and flip the pages. What colors continually pop up? What is your general impression of the color schemes? Are things dark and earthy or bright and cheery? You can try this in stores and boutiques as well (but watch your step!). Focus on the colors without getting caught up in the details of the items.

Materials

Pay attention to what is going on in the culture in terms of materials. Not just literally, as in what the designers are sending down the runway, but in a deeper sense,

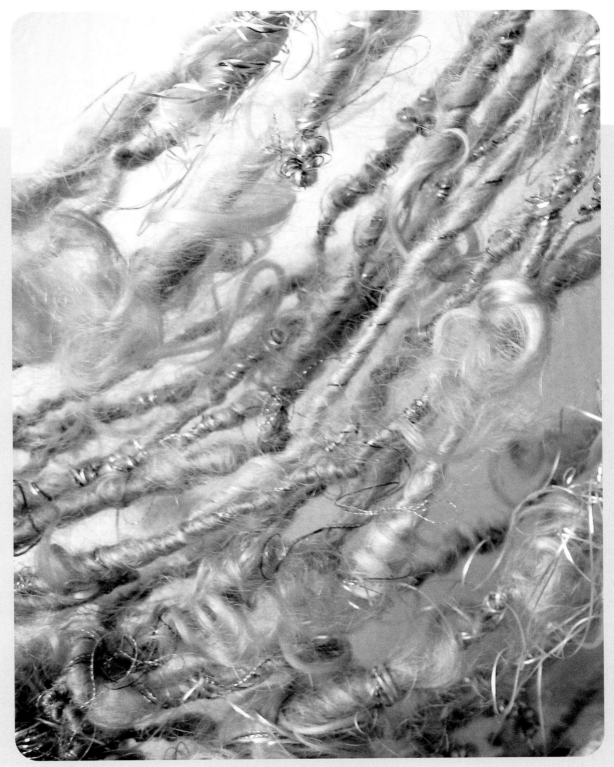

Fogbank, hand-dyed silver mohair with silver tinsel ribbon and sparkle.

Thick and thin merino single dyed in queasy green and spun with Halloween candy wrappers

less stream of *stuff* that our culture produces, review each material while asking yourself: *Can it be spun?*

Themes

Themes are never-ending. Literally. If you can't pluck a theme out of the swarming parade that is our culture, then you are a stone. You can find ideas in music, the news, holidays, public figures, history, media; the list is endless. Next time you see something on the news that you react to, ask yourself if it's worth working into a yarn. Monica Lewinski? Was that a navy polka-dot dress she saved? Try shredding up a blue dress and spinning it with some red, white, and blue. Throw in some little fireworks, or a match or two.

Find a theme from within the culture, then back it up with the material products that support that theme. Holidays are a perfect target for working this way. American culture has more contrived holidays than any other country and the mass of accessories that are produced to celebrate them is mind-boggling. Become a day-after-the-holiday clearance shopper and you will find some very interesting materials. You never know when a yarn is going to call for a neon green rubber Halloween spider or a petrified Easter peep.

such as what materials will fill the needs of our culture? With concerns over global warming and the health of the environment, for example, you may consider using *earth-friendlier* fibers and dyes. Are you into recycling? Take it to your yarn! Reuse old yarns by cutting them up and carding them into your wool. Before you throw out any old rags or clothes, ask yourself whether the material would make a nice yarn. Grocery bags, office paper, rubber bands, broken jewelry, wrappers, and more can be given a second life in your yarn.

Interesting materials can also be found outside the standard craft channels. Examine completely unrelated fields for spinning material. Electronic supply stores have a huge array of little wires, lights, bulbs, and other surprising things that can be worked into a yarn. Army surplus, office supply, and medical supply stores are all potential fiber bonanzas. As you sort through the end-

Paper Trail, Single-ply yarn in hemp, mohair, shredded office documents, and McDonald's burger bags

Fiber

Often times the very material and fiber that you use can be the direct source of inspiration for the yarn. Simply bringing out the potential that rests within the fiber itself is a natural and pleasurable way to create yarn. This process is dependant on *seeing* the fiber so you can respond to it. It is helpful to keep all of your fibers and materials stored on shelves or in containers that leave the fiber visible. This enables you to peruse all the possible ingredients for a yarn at one time. Try putting the materials next to each other to see how they interact; through this process you can create interesting combinations that you may not have been able to conceptualize.

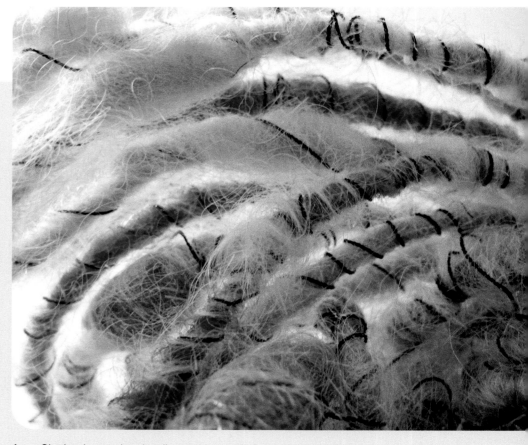

Aura, Single-ply yarn in miscellaneous uncarded wool surrounded by mohair and wrapped in novelty thread

Observation

Another important factor in making creative yarn is the simple act of observation. *Pay attention to the things that you usually don't pay any attention to.* This is where discovery happens. Instead of watching the yarn spin-

ning between your fingers, look at what the core thread is doing on the floor. Is it tangling? Making loops? Can they be integrated into the yarn? Instead of watching the fiber that you are spinning, look for the bits that fall to the floor. Why did they fall? Are they little interesting bits? Can they be collected and formed into something else? First, make an effort to see what we have been trained to block out and second, ask questions about it. This process will make you an innovator rather than just a spinner.

POPPIN' PILLS

This yarn is a perfect example of how open observation led to a new discovery. I was in the process of spinning the yarn for *Everything Nice* (page 40), which combined fine processed hemp, linen, and silk. Halfway through, my 7-month-old woke up and I had to leave the wheel and go nurse him. I sat idly on the couch with him; no television, no distractions. I was not thinking about anything or doing anything, just being in the moment. I was spacing out, just looking at my knee, when I noticed that I was covered in fiber from the spinning. I started picking at the fibers

Poppin Pills, Single-ply wool yarn with pills spun in

to get them off my pants, but they were sticky, so I rubbed my fingers together to get the fibers off. That didn't work, so I tried to transfer them to a denim pillow. Well that worked, but when I looked at the pillow I was surprised to see a perfect little sphere of fiber the size of a pea with two little long fiber tails coming out of it. *Cute!* I thought. Then I thought … hey wait, that *is* cute. So I started rolling balls out of the rest of the fiber from my pants and by the time my son was done nursing I had enough *pills* for a whole yarn. I went back to the wheel, put on a new spool, and spun a yarn with the little pills added in by trapping the fiber tails into the wool.

Hemp, silk *pills*

From Within

Just as the world around us is a never-ending source of inspiration, so too is our inner world. Our thoughts, emotions, perceptions, and ideas are excellent sources for creative yarns. From pure intellectual exercise to passionate expression, our internal landscape provides a bountiful resource from which to draw.

The Creative Concept

New techniques are sometimes discovered by accident and sometimes just happen, but another way to produce new yarn styles is to generate the concepts from your own mind. This is a more scientific approach to spinning. It works by forming a hypothesis and then testing to see whether that hypothesis is correct. It involves imagining a look you want, predicting how the fiber will behave, and then coming up with a way to make it happen. Then you actually try to make it happen. It may or may not work out like you predicted. But either way you learn how the fiber behaves in that situation. Then you take that knowledge and adjust your approach to accommodate the reality of what the yarn will do. Through imagining, testing, and adjusting, you can eventually create the effect you want. It is most important to remember when working this way that *there is always a way to do it*. You simply have to navigate through the trial and error process.

Memory and Experience

Our personal experiences are what combine to make us who we are. Drawing on your own story will imbue your yarns with your unique perspective. Though your own memories and experiences have personal meaning for you, they are also very interesting to other people because they allow others another glimpse into who you are. You can use your yarn as a medium to illustrate or commemorate certain things from your life experience, such as a specific time, event, or person.

We often keep a loved one's memory alive through certain family traditions, such as using their hallmark recipes or reciting their favorite joke. These are ritualistic actions that allow us to think about that person in a familiar, unencumbered way. Yarn making is the same kind of quiet, ritualistic activity that allows for this type of experience. For example, you can spin using materials that this person loved, or use their actual possessions, such as a favorite handkerchief, a piece of jewelry, or fiber dyed with beets from that person's garden. There are many ways to bring someone into your yarn. You can also bring yourself into your yarn in the same way, not just by using things that you like, but also by using things that you *are*.

Commentary

Yarn has traditionally fulfilled one of two roles: it's either functional or it's beautiful. But there is a whole

THE CREATIVE CONCEPT AT WORK

I wanted to create a single-ply yarn that had big loops coming off of it. I imagined that if I spun the yarn with a core thread, when I wanted a loop I could just spin a small section away from the core thread, then reconnect it forming a loop, and continue spinning. Well, instead of a loop I ended up with a twist. Cute, but not what I was looking for.

This forced me to ask more questions. Why is it twisting? (It was not set or plied.) How can I set it, but still have a single? (Hmmm.) I finally figured out that I would have to loosely spin a single, take it off the spool, and soak and set the twist, then wind it into a ball and spin it *again*, in the same direction along with a thread. Then I could make the loops, and since the single had been set, they would not twist on themselves.

I had met all the parameters that I set out: it was still a single ply, and it had untwisted loops. My original concept for how to do it was wrong, but by starting out with a wrong concept I eventually worked my way to the right one. The point is to start

somewhere, even if it does not work. If you can figure out why something failed, then you will figure out how to make it succeed.

different role that yarn can play, and that is as a medium to covey an idea. Decide what you want to say, then find the fiber, materials, and processes that will imbue your yarn with that meaning. Every material or object can convey a meaning. You can use the meaning or change the meaning of a specific material through the spinning process. For example, as I am writing this manuscript, we are at war. Many of the

soldiers lost are fathers. One could reclaim a soldier's field shirt, spin it into a yarn, and then knit a baby blanket. When people see that blanket, and know what it's made of, they would understand that through that yarn, a soldier might symbolically hold his baby. It is absolutely possible to transform something as inanimate as a yarn into something meaningful.

Trickle-Down Economics, The Yarn

by Jacey Boggs

February 6th is a birthday that I share with a pretty-faced man who would marry and divorce actresses, appear in over fifty movies, and oh yes, lead the United States through the bulk of the Cold War. Yep, I share a birthday with Ronald Reagan.

In the two class sessions that my college political science class took to cover Reaganomics, more derisively known as Trickle-Down Economics, the left-leaning, left lobe of the left side of my brain screamed and scooted my desk a little more to the left side of the room. Did anyone really think that trickle-down really trickled down? Ronnie did, and he employed it as he fought to bring down big government and prop up big business.

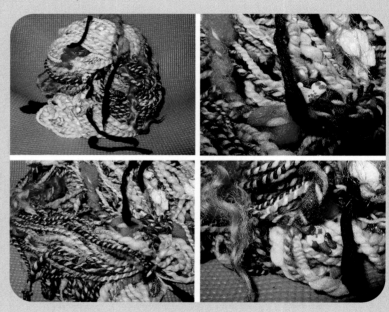

When I first thought of spinning a yarn called Trickle-Down Economics, I pictured it as something to knit from top to bottom, to represent the economic theory as a knitted piece. I envisioned it as a three-ply yarn: One to represent wealth, one to represent race, and one to represent gender. The wealth strand would start green and gold and fade out as it descended, while the race ply would begin white and quickly darken. The gender ply would represent a shift from men at the top to women at the bottom.

Utlimately, I couldn't make it work. What would make the money ply fade to? White would confuse the race ply at the proletariat level. How to represent gender without buying into the stereotypical demarcations of pink and blue?

So I decided on a two-ply yarn with one ply representing the Earth and the other incorporating everything else. The Earth part was easy. I painted some combed wool top (long strips of neatened wool) in earthy browns, sun yellows, and greens. Sitting at my spinning wheel I treadled out a lovely single yarn with enough extra twist so that it would hold a tight ply later when it would be twisted in the opposite direction with the race, gender, and wealth single. For that second single, I started with three ideas: shine, whiteness, and invulnerability to soiling, representing the elite class. I carded a lovely mixture of stark white soy silk for shine and bleached, superwash white wool for that clean quality. The results were white and shiny, but not quite rich enough, so into this single I spun cocoons of gold sparkly fiber that actually look like cocoons: I spun the tip of a small amount of gold sparkle accent fiber in the yarn, then held it out at a 90-degree angle and let it spin on while shaping with my fingers; the other end is then spun in with the main fiber to hold it in place. I added big blobs of uncarded recycled bottle fiber, a squeaky fiber ultra processed from beginning to end. From those plastic-fiber injections, 2-4 inch (5 to 10 cm) long, slender, irregular, hand-felted black strips drip like black gold (Texas tea), trickling down over the lower sections. Rather quickly, this whole section begins to have fewer and smaller gold cocoons, shorter oil strands, and bits and sprigs of color carded in. Of course, the superwash is slowly being replaced with non-superwash—stuff that when it gets dirty, is not so easy to wash. For those not following all the symbolism, the rich white guys exist mostly at the top of the knitted object, their oil slicks flow down on the folks below who have less money, and fewer resources, and more pigment in their skin. Slowly I card in more colors—reds, yellows, browns, and darker browns—until the white wool is only about 25 percent of the yarn, which more accurately represents the U.S. population.

Earlier in the week I'd made some tiny, tiny people out of polymer clay, all different colors and wearing tiny blue or gray jumpers. One guy is without an arm due to a tragic mill accident and one's bloody from a tumble with a union buster. They have tiny loops on their heads so that I could thread a bit of wool through and spin it right into the single, anchoring the beginning and end of the accent fiber. I extracted two little guns from my son's pirate set: these are spun alongside gobs of uncarded, nobbly, red wool erupting on the yarn like big blisters. Toward the bottom, blood-red locks cascade from the dark, textured yarn. What the yarn says: it can be a bloody, violent world the further you get from the privileged, superwash top.

I loaded the trickle-down ply and the earth ply on my lazy Kate and set to twisting them on each other. I plied the lower sections with the Earth single held straight and let the other wind onto it, barely showing the Earth through the darkly colored, heavily textured, and bloody mess. The closer I got to the superwash white at the top, the more I switched the tension. Finally, at the very top, every few feet I'd bring the Earth strand out at a 90-degree angle and let a little bump spin on the other single like a little estate view for those that can afford to just see the pretty parts of the world.

From top, clockwise: Handspun yarn for Ghost Town Zombie Hat, Geisha Scarf, Everything Nice Pill Box Hat

chapter 2
Start to Finish:

The following section features a collection of projects recorded from initial concept to finished piece, examining the process behind each one. Nice photographs of completed projects are deceptive. They represent the piece as an immaculate conception, almost as if the craftsperson had just opened her hands and a beautiful hat or scarf suddenly appeared out of a swirling cloud of stars and sparkles. As nice as that sounds, the reality is far from this illusion. In order to learn how-to, you must first learn how not-to. A lovely finished project can only be achieved through trial and error, steps and missteps, mistakes and successes.

In the following journal entries, you will see that the idea for the project continually changes and evolves. Things are added, things are discarded, and mistakes are made. This is where real learning happens. At the least, mistakes are bumpers that keep you on the right track; at best, they are the very gateways to invention. It is vital to work through the process; don't just discard a project when it starts going south. If you keep going south, you might end up going north, eventually.

Each project you create holds a different experience and a unique process. It is less a record of the creation of the piece than it is a mirror of your own progress as a craftsperson. If a project is plagued by one frustration after another, it may be a reflection not of the project's difficulty, but of your own. The process will let you know when you are on track or off. If you are rigid and cling to your ideas, the process may throw up one roadblock after another until *you* give. It's not a matter of creating what you want, but letting the creation guide you and become what it wants to be.

Ghost Town Zombie Hat

I was in Reno, Nevada, this weekend and there was a city-wide car show going on. There were tons of sappy, nostalgic, classic cars, cars dressed up like prom dates, and paintjobs that reminded me of over-the-top Florida manicures. But among the throngs of thumping cars, exhaust, and blinding chrome were a couple of absolutely incredible hot rods. They were completely rusted, mismatched, and patchworked from numerous old models, and were unbelievably cool. They had skulls on the engines and gear shifts and evil designs painted on so subtly you almost missed them.

They were what you would imagine rad zombies would drag race in down the main street of an abandoned ghost town. I am going to make a hat for zombie chicks to wear when they cruise around in their dead boyfriend's Rat Rod.

I've been collecting some good stuff for the Rat Rod hat. I found some little skull beads, tiny silver crosses, antique chains, and a vintage coverlet that I will use to line the hat. I also found a little gold-colored locket. I am going to scour the antique stores for some old photos—I need a ghost-ly image to put in there ... a long-lost love.

I also found some rusty and delicate parts while scrounging through my dad's shop. I'll spin these in as well. I am currently dying the wool but am having a little trouble getting the perfect rusty brown color. I'm on my third dye-batch!

I am also on the lookout for a big old black zipper that will run across the hat so it can zip on and off.

august 15

Unfortunately, there were no pictures while spinning this yarn. I did it at my camp and, like an idiot, forgot my camera. Needless to say, it actually went smoothly. I ripped up a tie-dyed linen skirt that made me look really fat. I had dyed it in graveyard grays and browns. It shredded very nicely with lots of stringy edges. I spent four hours spinning in all my skulls, crosses, and hardware and only ended up with 45 yards!! I don't think it will make the whole hat. I am spinning a single from gray/brown Icelandic wool and am debating whether to use that to extend the yardage. We'll see. I want to do either a big shadowy hood that unzips or an aviator-style hat.

august 21

Finally decided on a design for the hat. I went with the aviator look with a little asymmetry. I'll stripe it with a wool single dyed in the same colors so there will be enough yardage. I have a big zipper for the hood and I'll tear strips of the vintage fabric for the bow.

august 25

Final materials collected and the yarn is on the needles! I'm using big #17s [12.75 mm] and starting the bottom in a rib: knit 3, purl 3.

august 26

More knitting! Worked in the wool single and it matched really well. I'm starting to think this hat may be better without the lining and zipper, simplified. It depends on if it seems heavy once it's done. Hmmmm...

august 29

Hat done, but oh, man! Too big! Way, way too big. I'm going to stab myself in the eye with these needles! No, no. That's not going to help ... so I am ripping the whole hat out and starting over. The good part is that it turns out I won't need to use the wool single ... there will be enough Zombie for the whole hat. Little victories.

september 3

Almost done with the new smaller hat! Finally getting somewhere, here.

september 8

I'm cutting out the cotton lining and ribbon for the hat. I'll be dyeing the lining dark gray-brown and washing the ribbon in the washing machine so the edges fray nicely.

september 19

I had a snap disaster! My concept was to have the ribbons that hang off the earflaps snap on with big, heavy-duty metal snaps. That way, you could remove them for a guy's hat or snap them on for a more feminine look. Have any of you ever worked with snaps? It's kind of a pain, especially when they forget to write proper instructions on the box. I fooled around for an hour, went through at least eight snaps, and still could not get them to snap together. I finally realized, "Ohh, they're heavy-duty snaps and my fabric is lightweight!" DUH. But I still like the look of the big snaps and must have them. So I had to cut individual fabric strips, fold them over five times, and run the snap through all the layers. Essentially, I fooled the snap into thinking it's on a heavy-duty fabric. I trimmed the layers all around the snap and I will wash it again in the washing machine to fray the edges around the snap. It should actually look pretty cool, like a flower.

That was the first problem. The second problem is the strips are too short. They will tie into a nice bow, but there won't be much hanging down and I want the ribbon to trail down to waist level. I am almost out of fabric and will have to sew extension pieces on. Thankfully, this is a deconstructed project! Extensions will blend right in.

september 22

Done! Finally. So, here it
is. It's a basic dome
shape with ribbing
around the face, and
earflaps with removable
vintage cotton ribbons.
You can take off the
ribbon for a guy's hat. A
long haul, but worth it
this time. Now ... where's
that hot zombie guy?

Geisha Scarf

october 11

Check out these incredible handmade vintage flower buttons! These are very old. The stitching is all hand done. What to do with them? I'm not sure. They are just in time for Halloween with the colors ... but they are too cool to do anything too theme-ish. I think I will make a yarn that can be knit into a lacy scarf. The buttons halves will be dispersed throughout ... perhaps one could connect them up in different ways to make the scarf (shawl?) look different? Would it work? I don't see why not.

october 14

Mixed up a batt for this yarn. It is mostly latte-colored silk with some hemp and linen carded in. For texture I put some white and black silk noil. The black should look nice with the flower buttons. But I still think it's going to need something more, since there are only four buttons. I will go to the bead store and see if I can find anything ... maybe black pearls or orange crystals.

Finally found the right ingredients for this yarn. I was stuck because all I could picture was black, white, and orange and it just seemed too plain. But then I found this awesome '60s silk head scarf!! Hello? Check out those colors! The scarf was cool, but not quite cool enough to keep a scarf. So I shredded it. It was so very 1960's. But look at the flower buttons on it; a good and slightly weird mix. Next I found the great orange Indian beads and some bits of hand-dyed wool in complementary colors. I'll finish it off with the silver sparkle thread from France. Can't wait to get started on this one.

✢ From lower left, clockwise: '60s silk head scarf; shredded scarf; additional spinning materials

november 1

On the wheel! It's spinning up so cute, too. The shredded silk looks like little rosebuds and the size of them balances out the big buttons. I spun whole sections of the beads in at one time holding one end in my teeth! (Didn't have enough hands ....) Here are pictures on the bobbin, soaking, and stretching.

✢ From far left, clockwise: Spinning the button into the base yarn; spinning a strip of scarf fabric into a "rose"; string of beads after it is spun into the yarn; soaking the yarn in hot water to set the twist; stretching the yarn on a Twist-Away yarn tensioner

november 3

Yarn done! Here it is. Now I need to get knitting. I'm thinking of doing a very wide, short scarf. I saved some strips of the scarf to use as a fringe. I think I'll do an open pattern with lots of dropped stitches.

✛ Right: The finished yarn, ready to knit
Below: Beginning stages of knitting

november 19

It's on the needles. I have pulled it out twice and switched to little needles, and then back to large ones for the lacy look. I can't decide if it should be solid or lacy. I think I might start lacy and get more close knit as I go ... hmmm.

december 19

DONE!

Okay, that took forever! But here it is. It starts out really open on one end. I used big #13's and did lots of wraps, then dropped them. It has asymmetrical waves broken up by regular stockinette stitch. It gradually gets denser toward the middle of the scarf, with more stockinette and less open waves. Finally it graduates to a regular pattern of four knit rows, then two purl rows, repeated till the end. I also downsized needles as I went, ending up with #9's. The loose knit end has a fringe of Geisha yarn remnants and a few strips from the silk hankie. The other end has a fringe of solid hankie strips tied in bows and layers. It's thick so they look full and lively.

Tried my concept of connecting the buttons to shape the scarf— but nope! The scarf is knit too loose and it just pulls the strands out. Bummer! I guess I would have had to knit very tight for the connecting button idea to work. Next time ... for now I think it works like it is.

✝ Left: The finished scarf with extra scraps added for fringe (PHOTO BY KYLE PARKER). See page 206 for knitting instructions.

Everything Nice Pill Box Hat

I'm going to spin a sweet little yarn with these elements I scored at the thrift store the other day. It will be a mix of hemp and linen spun with shiny lumps of silk, vintage seam binding, embroidered lace, button loops, and these vintage flowers. The cones of thread were a great find; one is soft pink bubbly and the other is a natural thick and thin linen thread.

I will crochet it into a little pill box hat with a patent-leather band and bow ... if I can find some patent leather.

october 18

I cut each flower out and disconnected the leaves slightly ... to give me something to spin onto. I spun the fiber and threads around the narrow part of the leaf, then spun an inch or two before reconnecting to the next leaf. The idea here is that when I crochet it, I can hook into the yarn along the backside of the flower and make a loop. This will hook into the work and allow the flower to lay flat on the outside. Well, I hope it will work like that anyway.

I made tons of white silk bubbles in this yarn. I decided not to use the seam binding. I want this to be classier and less busy. Still looking for patent leather.

october 20

Yarn done! Yeah. Everything is going so slow lately! So here it is, and the flowers stayed nice and flat. I left all the trims out. I think I will use the vintage button loops to make a delicate edge at the bottom of the hat. The hemp/Tencel is fairly stiff ... so this will help give structure to the hat. Still need leather and a sweet hat pin.

november 4

I finally started the hat. I'm just doing a single crochet stitch all the way around. I will work this circle out until it has a circumference of 22 inches (55.9 cm), the same as my head, then I will stop increasing and work the sides down straight.

november 17

Well, this is as far as I got and I ran out of yarn. Instead of spinning more, I think I will look for a nice brown leather belt and make the bottom of the hat with it. Like the hat band, but in a more extreme way. The buckle can sit off center in the front. I'll have to spin a little more yarn so I have enough to attach the belt with ... to make belt loops, that is! I also need to go in with some thread and stitch down the flowers so the backsides don't show.

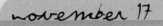

march 5

Well .... ok, did I ditch this project or what?! Forgive me, for it has been FOUR MONTHS since my last stitch! This just turned into one of those projects where I ran up on a glitch (ran out of yarn) and then just completely lost all my steam. This happens every now and then. I have that problem some of you may be familiar with: if I can't finish something fairly quickly it might never get done.

Sometimes, there is a positive side to letting things sit for a while. Different solutions may arise. This hat is a good example. Instead of a belt, I found some beautiful camel-colored soft, soft, soft leather in the thrift store (50 cents!). I cut a strip, folded it over, and made the headband. It was a little too plain so I went back to the original linen that the flowers came off of, and I cut a strip out of it for the little bow and band that wraps around the leather. This was that nice old kind of linen that is stiff and holds its shape when you work with it, so the bow perks up very nicely and the entire band has some nubbiness to it. All in all, I'm glad I shelved it. The leather and linen are much sweeter than a belt would have been.

✛ Right: Pill box hat with handspun yarn, suede and vintage linen
Jacket by Armour Sans Anguish

chapter 3
Free the Pattern!
THE YARN MADE ME DO IT

Working with handspun yarn provides a perfect opportunity to free yourself from the constraints of formal patterns by allowing the characteristics of the yarn itself to dictate the work's form. There are many ways to do this, and a few examples will follow, but the idea is to teach yourself to really look closely at the yarn, and let the details and eccentricities that you find there guide you in your creative process. Many people are hyper-focused on the act of knitting or crocheting, and oblivious to the yarn itself as they work through it. The following projects are intended to turn this tendency on its head, and take the focus off stitching and onto the yarn itself. This involves shifting from being a conscious stitcher/unconscious observer to being a conscious observer/unconscious stitcher. This process not only teaches you how to become aware of the subtle nuances and details of a yarn, but will also open you up to enhanced creativity.

Hippie Headband, Urban Hobbit Hat

Spin a yarn with an intrinsic color pattern and allow it to dictate the design as you crochet. Assigning basic crochet stitches to specific colors creates this wonderful project without difficulties.

Crochet Skills Required

Chain (ch)
Slip st (sl st)
Bobble
Single Crochet (sc)
Double Crochet (dc)

Size (HAT)

Length: 9" (23 cm)
Circumference: 21" (53.5 cm)

Materials

Hat: About 4 oz (113 g) prepared fiber, in 3-4 colors
Headband/Collar: About 1½ oz (40 g) prepared fiber in 3 or 4 colors
Size K/10½ (6.5 mm) crochet hook. Change hook size as necessary to accommodate your yarn and gauge.
Tapestry needle

Gauge

9 sc = 4" (10 cm) using size K/10½ (6.5 mm) crochet hook

A blend of Romney and Jacob fibers custom dyed with acid dyes.

The Fiber

Select 3 or 4 different colored fibers for this project. Any fiber or color combination will do. Prepare each color for spinning by separating the roving into easy-to-handle sections. Make all the sections different lengths to ensure that the pattern is not too regular.

The Yarn

Spin a simple thick-and-thin single, alternating the colors as you spin. Be sure to alternate the colors fairly evenly. You don't need to repeat an exact order throughout (i.e., red, blue, orange … red, blue, orange), but rather, alternate them randomly. This will make a more interesting pattern when you crochet the hat or headband. The color sections should vary anywhere from 6" to 36" (15–91.5 cm). Wash and tension your yarn, and allow to dry completely.

Simple thick-and-thin handspun single in several colors

Stitch and Color key

Blue – bobble(s)
Mustard – sl st
Light green – sc
Dark brown – dc

Hat

Ch 42 (or whatever number of chs will fit around the wearer's head), join chain into circle with slip st. Make sure the chain isn't twisted and the right side of work is facing outward. Using the stitch and colors listed above, crochet in rounds, changing the stitches according to the color in use. In other words: when the yarn color changes to blue, make one or more bobbles until the blue section is finished. If the next color is light green, work sc stitches until the color changes again. Don't worry if the color and stitches appear lopsided: if you alternated the colors fairly regularly when spinning, all will even out in the end.

tip: Transition stitches: If the yarn is a little of both colors, make a judgment as to which stitch will fit best into that particular spot.

Continue crocheting in the round until the hat measures about 6" (15 cm) from base chain. Begin to randomly decrease stitches about 2 stitches per round, every other round, for 4 rounds. Then decrease every round until the hat spirals closed.

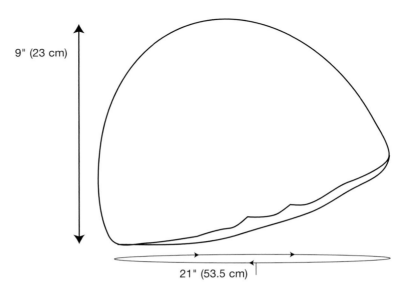

9" (23 cm)

21" (53.5 cm)

When to decrease will depend on your individual hat and the shape that your choice of stitches is creating. Use decreases to even out any lopsided parts.

NOTE: These instructions will make a basic cloche shape, as shown. Use your decreases to shape the hat differently, if you like. Don't decrease at all to make an ear hat (basically a square laid flat and seamed across the top. When worn, the corners make "ears"). Or, decrease very gradually after the first 6" (15 cm) to make a cone-shaped hat.

To make a smaller or larger hat, begin by crocheting a base chain long enough to loosely wrap around the wearer's head. Join the chain into a circle with slip st, then proceed as previously instructed.

Headband/Collar

Begin by crocheting a base chain long enough to wrap around the circumference of the intended wearer's head. Headbands usually have a slightly smaller circumference than hats; you don't want the headband too loose or it may slip over your eyes when you move your head! Join the base chain into a circle with slip st and work in color and stitch patterns same as hat. When headband/collar measures about 3"–4" (7.5–10 cm) from base chain, finish off where the last stitch will blend in naturally.

That's it! Now you have a perfect hat to wear under a bridge or to the Renaissance Fair tailgate party.

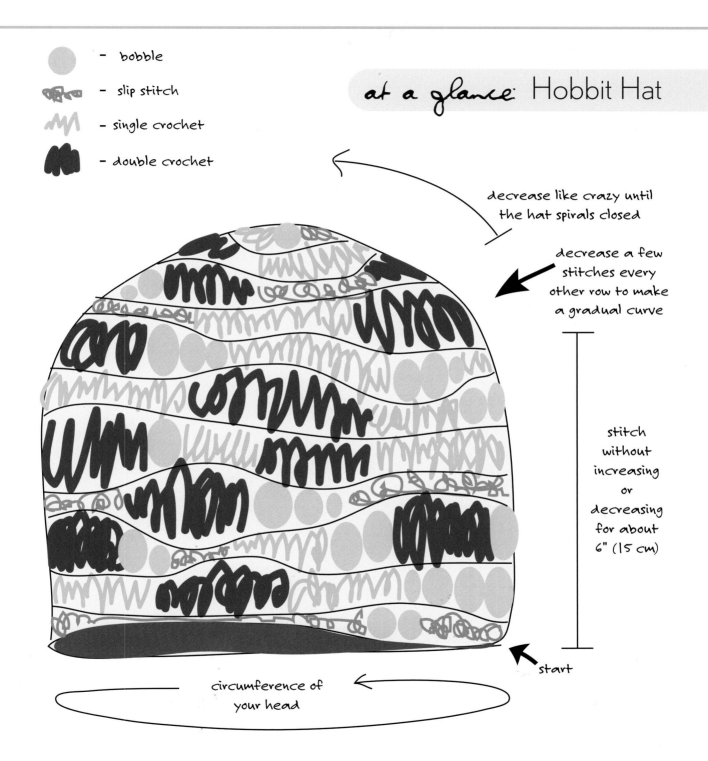

- bobble
- slip stitch
- single crochet
- double crochet

at a glance: Hobbit Hat

decrease like crazy until the hat spirals closed

decrease a few stitches every other row to make a gradual curve

stitch without increasing or decreasing for about 6" (15 cm)

start

circumference of your head

Nozzlers

Nozzlers, or "fiber-travelers" as the ancients called them for their ability to wiggle in and out of the many dimensions of the universe, are an elusive and clever spirit creature. They do not actually exist in a solid state, but are more like dense spots within the fabric of the universe; semi-gelled masses of energy and vibration. The ancients discovered a way to conjure these travelers out of the energy field and manifest them in a solid form. Once manifested, the ancients could seal them forever in their earthly bodies through a process of heat and friction known as *fibration*. The shape that each Nozzler would take was unknowable until that particular individual arrived on this plane. Each energy/vibration unit is unique and has its own density and frequency, and when it is conjured into the physical world, the form it takes is the physical version of its energy state. The ancients observed this phenomenon with great enthusiasm, and greeted the emerging new forms with unbounded excitement.

Once sealed in an earthly body, a Nozzler would become a companion and trusted advisor to the human who conjured it. It was believed that every human had a Nozzler counterpart on a separate plane and that no human would be wholly complete until she was united with his or her spirit Nozzler.

The ceremony to conjure a traveler from its place in the fabric of the universe is a process that takes time and focused energy. Humans must open their hearts and reach across the planes to connect with their true spirit Nozzlers. If the human is clouded or unfocused, he or she may conjure the wrong traveler (not his or her own), and the outcome of this scenario is … unspeakable. Every major catastrophe in human history can be traced back to humans meddling with someone else's spirit Nozzler. And until all humans are united with their true Nozzlers, there will not be peace on Earth. So, the ancients insist, one must be of true and honest heart

when conjuring one's spirit Nozzler. In addition, one must follow all the steps of the ceremony with the utmost of care and attention, lest a Nozzler not be transported to this realm intact—a blunder that has cost many a civilization a great deal.

Manifesting Ceremony
The Flesh

The ancients discovered that there were only a few materials that could be used to permanently house the spirit of the Nozzler. Only the fiber from a sacred sheep or goat would suffice; no plant or manmade fiber could detain the Nozzler in this world. And so it came to be that the flesh of the Nozzler had to be spun from the fibers of sheep or goats.

The Yarn

The ancients also discovered that a Nozzler in energy form would only respond to a call transmitted through a very special vibration. This could be created by the spinning action of a spindle or spinning wheel. Thus, the ancients spun the fiber into a yarn that could be made into the body of the Nozzler. The whirling, spinning, and twisting sent out a perfect note that stretched across the great divide and awoke the Nozzler from its dormant state. The spinning must be kept up long enough for the spirit Nozzler to find its way onto the earthly plane. Once awoken, the traveler sends messages across the universe to its human and silently instructs the human how to make the exact yarn that will become its body.

Spinning

The ancients advised the examination of many wools and goat fibers before making the intuitive selection for

your spirit Nozzler. Begin by spinning a single strand. Once you have sent out the initial signal, await a reply from your spirit Nozzler. You will receive silent nudges to add this color or that, or to change fibers or thicknesses. Some Nozzlers will call for long uncarded locks and some may want little tidbits of manmade creations to embellish their earthly bodies. Whatever they ask for, spin it, even if it does not seem reasonable to you. The Nozzler knows what it needs to complete its true physical form. The ancients found that most Nozzlers needed several bobbins worth* of yarn to properly manifest.

Set the Code

The spinning action of the spindle and the silent commands of the Nozzler are embedded in the newly spun yarn. This information is the code for the shape of the Nozzler and must be permanently set into the yarn, lest it be lost. Submerge the yarn in a bath of hot water for a half hour. Remove the yarn and squeeze

The Nozzler body before the fibration process

or spin out the excess water. The code must further be ingrained by a stretching process. Hang the yarn to dry with a heavy object cradled in its base, or place it upon a sacred stretching device.

Take Shape

Once the yarn is dry, select a sacred crochet hook and begin crocheting a simple chain or circle. Clear your mind of all thoughts and open your heart to receive the instructions from your spirit Nozzler. The Nozzler will dictate the pattern of the body; simply do as you are guided to do. The ancients found that most Nozzlers needed their humans to change stitches with every new color section in the yarn. They also usually require the human to change directions, sometimes crocheting in spirals, sometimes flat and sometimes in the round. Throughout all time, there have never been two Nozzlers the same, but there is one rule that each human must adhere to: the body must be a hollow, fully enclosed, three-dimensional shape. A Nozzler cannot inhabit a flat body. The body must be an enclosed space, as it is in that space that the spirit must be housed.

Fibration

Once the crocheting of the body is complete, place it in a sacred washing machine set to hot, anoint with ¼ cup soap, and commence the Fibration Ceremony. After one full cycle, remove the body and see whether it has completed the trans-

formation process. If it is still not wholly fused or has spaces, or if your spirit Nozzler says it is not done, place it back into the sacred machine for another full cycle.

Inhabitation

Remove the body from the sacred machine. Unfold the body so that its shape can be seen. Look for a discreet place and make a 3" (7.5 cm) incision. Using a soft clean fiber such as wool or cotton, begin to fill the body with fiber. The spirit and energy of the Nozzler already inhabits the form; this fiber is simply an earthly metaphor for the spirit of the Nozzler. Fill every space tightly with the fiber, ensuring that every little bump and shape that can be protruded, is; a Nozzler needs every part that it called for in order to fulfill its role as guardian, companion, and advisor. Using a darning needle and matching yarn, close the incision. Complete the ceremony by trimming any tangles or lint that adhered to the body during fibration.

The author's true spirit Nozzler

With this, the Manifestation Ceremony is complete. You have now been joined in this world by your Nozzler counterpart, who will serve as your guide and confidant. Be aware, say the ancients and do not have an expectation of what your guide will be like. They are what you need, not necessarily what you want. Some are sweet, some are mischievous, some have split personalities, but, say the ancients, each will play a very important role in the life of its human.

Several bobbins worth translates to approximately 200 yards in our day and age.

Coach: This little monster is made from my husband's very first yarn. It was a lumpy, bulky to thread-thin single in gray mystery wool plied with a cotton string. It was spastic, extreme, soft and coarse, and … totally wonderful. It hung around for a long time, quietly on its hook. Then for some reason one day when I walked past it, it just seemed to scream: crochet me! I was 9 months pregnant. I grabbed the skein and my hook and sat down and made this little monster.

As I finished the last stitch in the pupil of the last eyeball, I went into labor. I named him Coach and he went to the hospital and sat in the delivery room, giving quiet strength and reassurance with his crooked eyes and over-spun eyebrows. The big chunk of wool that somehow escaped getting any twist became Coach's big outstretched paw, waving, waiting for a big high five. This is exactly what this yarn was supposed to be. My husband's first yarn creation became the witness to our first creation.

chapter 4

Nontraditional Spinning Techniques

MATERIALS AND INSTRUCTIONS

No Such Thing as Ugly:
Some Thoughts on Essence and Purpose

The woman who taught me to spin once said that there is no such thing as an ugly yarn. The more handspun yarn I see, the more I'm convinced of this truth. No hand-created yarn is good or bad per se; it just is what it is. It is a matter of recognizing the essence of the material that you are spinning and allowing that essence to influence you as you spin. Be in tune with your material. Observe it rather than dominate it. Do not impose your will onto it, but rather let it form itself as you spin it. You have to find the balance between maintaining enough control to make a sound yarn while letting go enough to let the material take the shape it wants to take. This is the goal. It's really not about the yarn itself at all. It is about finding that fine line, a razor-thin groove, and zipping along it, spinning in a space where there is no control but nothing is out of control. Spinning in perfect balance, where both you and the material come together in a seamless moment and a strand is formed that is exactly what it is supposed to be.

(Continues on page 58)

That is the first step in this process. Allow the material to be what it wants to be and bring its essence to the forefront. The next step is to find the right *purpose* for the yarn. Every yarn has its own unique qualities, and if it is used for the right purpose it will make sense. It can be something, or it can just be itself. Again, it is a matter of letting go. Put control aside for a while and just ask the question: "What does it want to be?" The answer is always right there if you can remove yourself enough to see it.

Take It and Run

The following yarn techniques are only a few in an infinite realm of possibilities. They were discovered through trial and error, observation, and a little dumb luck.

Use them to learn how to do some basic things, but, like a baton race, take them and push them to the next step. Let these exercises be a gateway to your own invention. *Spin like this* to learn what these techniques have to offer, but at the end of the day the goal is to learn to *spin like you.*

Skills Needed

The following yarn instructions assume a basic knowledge of spinning on the part of the reader. Spinners should be able to spin balanced, even singles and know the basic mechanics of plying.

Capture the essence of the material — recycled sari silk.
Sari Salad, Handspun single-ply yarn, by Pluckyfluff

Equipment Needed

WHEEL Many of the following techniques can be done on a standard spinning wheel. A few require large orifice wheels (½"+ [1.3 +] cm) or quill attachments. These instructions are not written for the drop spindle; however, it's worth trying them with a spindle if that's your preferred spinning tool.

CARDERS Heavy-duty hand carders or drum carder.

THREADING HOOK The tool inserted into the orifice to pull the leader yarn through the orifice in order to attach to the fibers.

On Fiber

It is important to establish a relationship with a fiber producer whose farming philosophy is a good fit with your feelings on the issues. Some people are ambivalent on the subject, while others take painstaking steps to research the production practices of fiber sources. Whatever your position, find suppliers that you feel good about supporting. Most farmers are happy to talk about their philosophies if you show an interest. The story on the opposite page is an example of one farm's adoption-focused approach to raising a fiber flock.

On Handedness

The following instructions will not specify which hand to use to perform a specific task. This is because spinning is *not* a handed activity. Each spinner will naturally use one hand or the other to draft, wrap, hold plying threads, etc., and each person is unique. The best way to approach these techniques is to read the instructions, picture what is supposed to happen, and then try it using the hand that feels most natural. If it's not working, switch hands until you find what is most comfortable.

Terms

BASE YARN The straightforward yarn that serves as a foundation and has elements added to it. For example, in a beaded yarn, the yarn itself is the base yarn, and the beads are the additions. Many of these techniques feature simple yarns (base yarns) with interesting elements spun onto them.

CORE MATERIAL A thread or material spun inside the yarn. A core thread is used as a base and fiber is spun around it.

For Best Results

Read all instructions through from start to finish at least once before starting.

ANIMAL FRIENDLY WOOL?? YOU BET!

by Sandy Ryan
Homestead Wool and Gift Farm
www.homesteadwoolandgiftfarm.com

Step back from the animal-friendly wool debate for just a moment. There are many meanings to the much-coined "animal friendly" phrase—and just as many slants on what is right or wrong when it comes to raising sheep.

While our approach to a spinning flock is not something that works for everyone, you should know that there IS indeed animal-friendly wool available—much more than you think!

Odey, flock member from Homestead Wool and Gift Farm

Our flock has been built with sheep and fiber animals that needed help and a place to live out their lives—and many we purchased that we "couldn't resist"! We believe animal friendly means our animals are treated humanely, with the utmost consideration and respect for their physical and mental wellness. They are never sold once they join our flock, we do not eat them, and they are not allowed to have babies (unless they arrive here pregnant, of course!). If we let them have babies, we would end up with 500 sheep in a hurry, mainly because we could never bear to part with a single one of them. They are our family and are treated as such.

This leads to one age-old question of whether it is humane to neuter sheep. We do neuter our male sheep; however, we do use the most current pain medications to keep them from hurting. The surgery is done early in life when it is least stressful for them, and this helps them be more mannerly during their lives and avoid future health problems.

Another question circles around shearing sheep, which we believe to be crucial to a sheep's health and well-being. Just think what could happen if we never washed our hair or never cut it—not too comfy, right? Unshorn sheep are prone to horrible problems, from fly strike to heat stroke, sores, crawly bugs, and more—even the inability to move about because of a tangled, matted fleece. My son and I recently spent over an hour helping a friend rescue a little sheep that had never been shorn. Her fleece consisted of nearly 20 pounds (9.1 kg) of matted filth. We had to use a bolt cutter to remove her collar, but underneath all that, there was a good 2 inches (5 cm) of wool to keep her warm through the winter. She actually was so happy to have that mess taken away that she fell asleep while we were shearing her.

PIERCE SCHMIDT PHOTOGRAPHY

While it is important to shear, it is equally, if not more important, to have a kind, caring shearer who is skilled and careful with the sheep. We have several sheep who have had broken limbs or who have arthritis. Even our little sheep Molly is missing part of her back leg.

Shearing is accomplished by setting the sheep on its hinder and carefully turning the sheep to remove the entire fleece. Our shearer is careful not to cut them with the clippers, and the whole process is over in about five minutes or less per sheep. The gift of a great shearer cannot be measured. Keeping the sheep calm and comfortable and cradling them to keep them safe from traumatic injuries or experiences is crucial.

We have acquired a very diverse group of sheep that will happily pay their way by providing us with entertainment, happiness, and, of course, fleece for the rest of their lives. There are many special needs or homeless sheep out there that just need a safe place to be. Some are victims only of a changing family situation, others have had terrible things happen to them (just like any other animal), but there are also many people who accept them unconditionally and love them no matter the disability, age, or special needs. Animal-friendly wool? You bet!

Carding and Crazy Carding

For me, the single most important piece of equipment to have on hand when creating beautiful yarn is a drum carder. It is even more important than a wheel, because yarn spun from a home-carded batt will have ten times the character as yarn spun from commercial roving.

I would rather have a drop spindle and a drum carder than a fantastic wheel and commercial roving. Hand carders are okay, but it takes a lot of time and effort for me to produce a small amount of useable fiber.

A drum carder is a substantial investment, but in the long run it will save you plenty of money by allowing you to purchase raw or uncarded fleece, which you can process yourself. You can buy 4 or more pounds (1.8 kg) of raw Merino fleece for the same price as *1* pound (0.4 kg) of commercially-processed Merino combed top. In addition, hand-processed fiber retains much more texture and loftiness. (See the Advice Center, page 145, for instructions about washing raw wool.)

Traditionally, carding has been used to prepare the fiber for spinning by separating the locks and grooming them into one direction. The goal was to get every little lump out and generate a fiber that would spin evenly and quickly. The carder had always been an instrument for taming the fiber, but no more! A drum carder in the hands of a creative thinker can be a tool for unleashing the most stunning and unusual qualities from a wide range of fibers and materials.

Think of a carder as a mixer rather than a tamer, and a batt as a creation in and of itself. All of your color, texture, and material choices can be put together in the carding process. The rest is easy … just spin!

tip: *What type of carder should I buy? Almost any drum carder will suffice, but look for medium to heavy teeth and an enclosed drive mechanism. Any exposed gears are likely to collect fiber and get clogged, and an exposed drive band may crawl off its tracks when working particularly thick material through the carder.*

Mixed fixings layered on carder tray feeding the licker in roller, and then onto the larger drum roller for carding.

Mohair *bread* (base layer)

Above: Uncarded fiber. Wool, mohair, cotton, and Lincoln locks.

Fixings, clockwise from top left: Recycled silk, cut mohair yarn, shredded money, lace, recycled denim, black silk noil, felted orb, sparkle, aluminum fiber, threads, sequin trim, cut lace-weight yarn, and tinsel

Crazy Carding

Thick 'n' thin single spun from a crazy-carded batt by Pluckyfluff. The yarn includes wool, mohair, sequins, recycled silk, cut threads and yarns, shredded money, semi-felted wool, silk noil, Lincoln locks, recycled denim, Tencel, lace, and sparkle.

Crazy carding is the perfect way for spinners, including novice spinners, to make highly unusual and creative yarns easily. The concept is to put as many different colors, textures, and materials as possible into one batt, then spin it into a simple thick 'n' thin single. Very little skill is needed on the spinning end, and creating the batt is a fun and liberating exercise. Crazy carding integrates absolutely any fiber or material that will fit through the carder's drums, including silk waste, felted wool, tinsel, sequins, fabric bits, plant fibers, yarn, sparkle, silk noil, cotton, or pretty much anything else you could imagine. Be prepared to push your carder's capabilities to the limit. It is normal for the machine to card very clumpy at first, and it will be hard to crank.

Make a Sandwich!

The basic process for crazy carding is to combine several different ingredients at a time and send them through the carder in a thick clump. This will

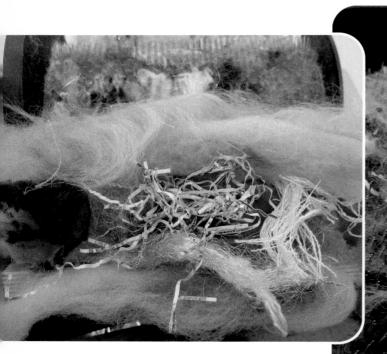

Sandwich: Bottom layer of wool roving and mohair, fixings in the middle (shredded money, sparkle, thread, blue silk cap, black silk noil, aluminum fibers, and red semi-felted wool), top layer of yellow mohair. Card this all at once!

Fiber in the drum

MINI BATTS!

Do not discard the fibers that are collected on the small drum—this is pure fiber gold! Remove the fiber from the small drum and use this mini-batt to add highly textured lumps or nubs to your yarns. This is a great way to make a complemetary yarn to your crazy-carded single. Spin a single from the big batt, then spin another yarn in solid-colored roving and add lumps from the mini-batt to make a coordinated set.

cause the materials to be minimally blended together and will preserve many heavy textures.

Short-fiber materials tend to get caught up in the teeth of the small drum and do not usually make it into the batt. To avoid this, sandwich all the short fibers or other unusual materials between layers of longer stapled fibers, such as mohair or processed roving (see top left image). Visualize making a sandwich: spread a flat layer of mohair or roving out first as the bread, add uncarded locks (lettuce), semi-felted wool (tomatoes), sparkle and silk noil (salt and pepper), top with another layer of mohair/roving bread, and send it through the carder!

Mini-batt

Below:
Crazy-carded batt

Repeat this process, adding different *fixings* in each sandwich. Sandwiches should be about 3 - 4" (7.5 – 10 cm) thick. Card until the large drum is full.

NOTE: Only card the batt once. Over-carded batts tend to lose their interesting textures.

Spin!

Remove the crazy-carded batt from the carder. Starting from the outside edge, pull off spinnable strips and spin a simple thick 'n' thin single. Do not over-draft. Allow the lumps, bumps, tangles, and textures to remain.

Thick 'n' Thin

Thick 'n' thin yarns are both lovely in and of themselves, but they also add an interesting dimension when plied. The trick to spinning thick and thin: it's all in the draft! First, separate your batt or roving into easy-to-spin sections, then begin spinning a simple single. Thick 'n' thin yarn is almost painfully simple to create:

Thin = draft
Thick = don't draft (or draft less)

Materials
4 oz (113 g) any fiber, carded in batt or roving form

tip: Wool is the easiest fiber to use while learning this technique.

Basically, thick 'n' thin yarn is the result of a bad drafting technique. Instead of drafting the fiber evenly, keeping the same volume of fiber at all times, try to draft irregularly. Stop drafting the fibers completely for a few inches (centimeters) to create a thick area, then draft the fiber out significantly, thereby creating a very thin spot in the roving. Spin through the thick and thin spots at the same speed—this will result in less twist in the thick spots and more twist in the thin spots.

tip: Tension is important for spinning thick 'n' thin yarns. The tension must be set right in the middle; if it's too light, the thin sections will severely over-twist, but if it's too tight, the yarn will pull apart in the thicker spots.

Softserve, 50/50 wool and mohair blend with black silk noil

Soft-Spun Singles

Not every fiber works well for this technique. Hand- or drum-carded batts are the most effective because the carding adds air and loft to the fiber. Look for fibers that are not too stiff or dense; use wool, mohair, and silk (silk is best if blended with about 20 percent downy fiber, wool, or mohair). Fibers such as hemp, linen, and cotton do not lend themselves to soft spinning as readily. Short fibers should be blended with longer fibers for stability.

Materials

4 oz (113 g) hand- or drum-carded batt

This technique is simply a loftier version of the standard thick 'n' thin single (see page 68). Begin spinning a thick 'n' thin single as you normally would. Now increase the tension slightly and permit the thick sections to be a little thicker than those usually found in a standard thick 'n' thin yarn. Allow about 30-40 percent *less* twist than normal. The idea is to have just enough twist to hold the yarn together, but not so much twist that the yarn feels dense. It is very important to spin this yarn as thick 'n' thin, because the thin sections will attract the twist and give the yarn structure, while the thick parts will barely accept any twist, giving the overall appearance of softness.

Spin until the bobbin is full. Soak the skein and then *gently* set the yarn while lightly tensioned.

Candy Striping

This technique is basically reversed core spinning. Instead of spinning with a thread on the inside of the yarn, the thread wraps around the outside. Instructions provided here are a simplified version from Pluckyfluff, *Handspun Revolution*.

Materials

4 oz (113 g) fiber
Thread for striping or lace-weight yarn

Spin!

Attach the striping thread and fiber and begin spinning a basic single. Spin, holding your hands as you normally would, except have the thread running through the palm of your hand (not the drafting hand) as you spin. To ensure that the thread sits on top of the yarn and does not get twisted inside, spin the wool but allow the thread to drift on for a split second behind the twist, laying it on top. You can use your pinkie finger to hold the thread and prevent it from getting tangled in the roving as you spin.

at a glance Candy Striping

Orifice

Allow the striping thread to spin on just after the base yarn has been spun.

Wire-core yarn holding its shape

Wire-Core

Materials

4 oz (113 g) wool roving
100 yds (91.5 m) fine-gauge wire

Wire can be found at any craft or hardware store. The gauge depends on how stiff you want your final yarn to be. Look for a wire that will easily hold its shape, yet bends easily.

Spin!

Attach the wire to the leader string on your wheel along with some roving. Begin spinning as you would with a core thread. Hold the wire with one hand and guide the wool onto the wire with the other. The wool should easily twist around the wire, covering it completely. Make sure the tension is set to medium or low-medium/low so that the yarn is not pulled onto the bobbin before it is sufficiently covered.

Wire-core yarn by Kathy Foster.

Soak in hot water, spin out excess water, and set the yarn.

This technique was contributed by Kathy Foster, www.electrickat.com

Jumbo yarn by Drucilla

Jumbo Yarn

This technique works best with combed-top commercial rovings spun on a bulky spinning wheel.

Materials

16 oz (454 g) combed-top roving
Striping thread or lace-weight yarn

Fiber Prep

Tear the roving into easy-to-handle sections about 36" (91.5 cm) long. Do not make the strips of roving too thin. Split the roving in half lengthwise but no smaller! This yarn is going to spin up bulky, up to 2" (5 cm) in diameter in the thick spots.

Spin!

Attach your fiber and striping thread and begin spinning a normal single (see "Candy Striping," page 72). Spin this fiber as you would a thick 'n' thin single, except with this difference: *do not draft at all* for the thick parts. Draft normally for the thin spots. The thick areas should be about as thick as your thumb and constitute about 70 percent of the entire skein.

Soak in very hot water for about 20 minutes, spin out excess water, and set the yarn on a yarn stretcher.

This technique is courtesy of Drucilla.

Silk and camel thick and thin single *wrapped* in a delicate linen thread

Right: Self-striping mohair and rainbow wool single with uncarded cotton sections *wrapped* in black/purple novelty thread

Wrapped Yarn

This yarn is basically the opposite of core spinning. Instead of wrapping the fiber around a core thread, the thread gets wrapped around the fiber. The thread is now a decorative element instead of a structural one. Choose a thread that looks good with your fiber or has an interesting shape, pattern, or color. Any fiber will work for this technique.

Materials

4 oz (113 g) fiber or roving for base yarn
*300 yds (275 m) novelty thread or lace-
     weight yarn*

Spin!

Attach your roving and the thread to the leader and begin spinning a normal single. Spin a few inches (centimeters) with the thread spun into the fiber so that it is anchored. Now, take your hands off the thread and only spin the roving. As you spin, allow the thread to wind onto the yarn unencumbered between you and the orifice. Pretend that the thread is not even there. It will wrap around and around the yarn near the orifice. Sometimes it will backtrack on itself, sometimes it will jump ahead. For the most part you can just let it do its thing. Occasionally, however, it may get stuck in one spot and need to be guided forward or backward. The *most important thing* is to make sure that the thread is not under too much tension. Make sure it's on a cone or a spool that allows the thread to wind off easily without getting hooked up. If you have a ball of yarn or thread, put it in a bucket just under the orifice. The thread should have just the slightest bit of tension, as too much will just create knots.

Repeat this process continually until the bobbin is full.

NOTE: You can also wrap strategic spots in the yarn instead of the entire length. Use this technique to create small areas of texture within the yarn. (See inset photo on page 78.)

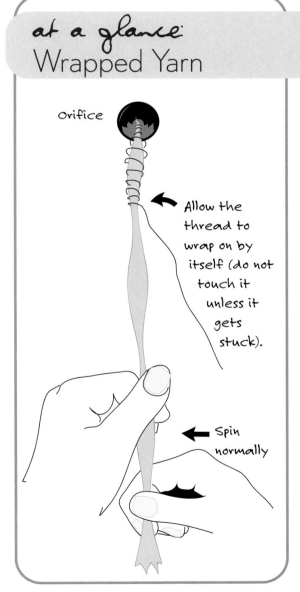

at a glance
Wrapped Yarn

Orifice

Allow the thread to wrap on by itself (do not touch it unless it gets stuck).

Spin normally

Backstage, handspun cassette tape on commercial wool core, by Pluckyfluff

Rock On: SPINNING CASSETTE TAPE

There are many possible techniques for integrating this material into your yarn. Spin the tape into flowery tangles or cut strips of tape to make shiny spikes. Drucilla pioneered this material originally with a bold striping technique (see "Candy Striping," page 72).

Materials

4 or 5 cassette tapes
100 yds (91.5 m) medium-weight yarn
  in brown/black

This technique came out of a strange customer request—she wanted a knit hat that would look like patent leather. While digging around in my fiber stash for something suitable, I stumbled across an old, strung-out cassette tape that was tangled in my mohair. I was just about to toss it when the light glinted off of it just enough to catch my eye. Slightly shiny ... warm brown color ... clean texture ... patent leather-esque? Definitely!

Fiber Prep

Select 3 or 4 full length cassette tapes. I find head-banging rock works well, but classical tends to have the darker colored tape. Make sure you look closely at the tape color; it runs from light brown (Julio Iglesias and easy jazz mixes tend to run in this shade) to very dark and almost slate. The more successful the band, the higher the quality, and the darker the color, of the tape. For example, early Metallica tapes tended to be light in color, as in *Ride the Lightning*, but by the time ... *And Justice for All* was recorded, the tape was the perfect dark brown color.

NOTE: This rule did not seem to apply to AC/DC. I could not find a single AC/DC tape in a suitable color. So keep that in mind when you are cruising through your relatives' closets for old tapes.

Core Yarn

Choose a soft commercial core yarn in a color that will blend in with the cassette tape. Soft commercial wool singles seem to work best. The finished yarn tends to retain enough softness and flexibility to be wearable.

Tapes

Prepare the tapes for spinning by pulling the tape out from the bottom of the cassette for about a yard (meter). Use scissors to cut the loop. Repeat this process with 4 or 5 cassettes. You will be spinning 2 strands of tape at a time.

Extra bulky thick 'n' thin Merino single striped in cassette tape by Drucilla

Close-up view of yarn

Spin!

Connect the core yarn and 2 *strands* of cassette tape to the leader string and begin spinning a single. Set the tension somewhere in the middle to light side. Hold the core yarn directly in front of you. It should go into the orifice head on, not at an angle. Let the cassette tape wind on from the side, at almost a 90-degree angle to the core yarn. As you are spinning, pull long sections of the tape out of the cassette and let it loosely wrap around the core yarn. As soon as it's wrapped, allow the yarn to wind onto the bobbin. Do not wind the tape on

very tightly or it will make a very stiff final yarn that will not be wearable. However, every few inches (5-7.5 centimeters), allow a small section to wrap tightly. This serves as little anchor points, keeping the tape from sliding around too much.

If you find that the tape is striping the core yarn instead of wrapping around it, your tension is too tight. Hold the yarn back from entering the orifice until it is wrapped in a nice, solid, even pattern. Repeat this process until the bobbin is full.

Set the Twist

Unwind the yarn from the bobbin and onto a niddy noddy. Prepare a hot water bath. Remove the skein from the noddy and submerge in the water bath. Soak the skein for *only* 2-3 minutes! You don't want to damage the tape material. Remove and *gently* squeeze out excess water by hand. Place the skein in the washing machine, set on the Spin cycle, and spin until all water is removed. Stretch the skein on a tensioner or between some chairs. Use sufficient tension to make the skein taut, but don't overstretch.

Shredded Paper Yarn

Materials

*3 oz (85 g) shredded paper (from a paper-
    shredding machine)*
4 oz (113 g) fine processed hemp
½ oz (14 g) white mohair
¼ oz (7 g) sparkle
Silk thread or fine gauge wire
Drum carder

Card the hemp, mohair, sparkle, and shredded paper together in a drum carder (see "Crazy Carding," page 64, for carding instructions). Tearing off spinnable strips from your batt, spin a simple thick 'n' thin single. Spin the thread or wire along with the roving for extra structure. Many of the paper bits will fall out during spinning, and this is normal. Expect roughly half the paper to make it into the actual yarn.

Once the bobbin is full, wind the yarn onto the niddy noddy. Soak in hot water for *45 seconds*, spin excess water out, and stretch yarn to set the twist.

Nubs are very easy to make and have many variations and uses. A nub is made by spinning a small chunk of roving or fiber onto a forming yarn at a 90-degree angle. (These are different from slubs, which are incidental lumps that naturally occur in the roving while spinning.)

Nubs and Cocoons

Nubs
Materials
4 oz (113 g) fiber for base yarn
½ oz (14 g) contrasting fiber for nubs

NOTE: You can use any fiber for nubs: wool, silk, sparkle, fiber scraps, etc. Don't be afraid to experiment!

Fiber Prep
Select the fibers you want to use for the nubs. Pull out pieces of fiber about 2 x 1" (5 x 2.5 cm) from your fiber supply (this amount makes a peanut-sized nub). Draft the edges out a little so it will grab onto the base yarn easily.

Spin!
Begin spinning a singles yarn. When you are ready to add a nub, stop the wheel and draft your base yarn roving out until you have a thin section. Pinch the drafted end of the nub fiber to this thin section of roving and resume spinning. Allow the drafted end of the nub fiber to catch in the thin section of the base fiber.

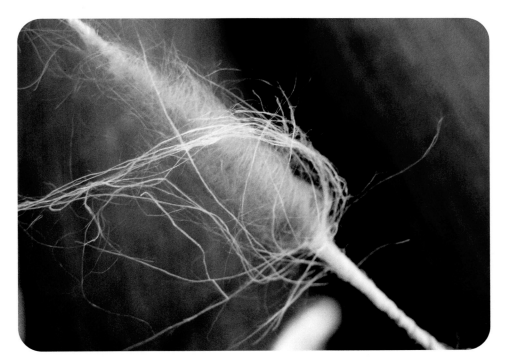

Just-spun wool nub on hemp yarn. Note: The wispy fiber shown here is unspun hemp added while tacking in the end of the nub.

As you spin, the nub section will want to wrap around the base yarn.

tip: Don't wait for the nub fiber to get pulled on, as the pull is too light to detect. Instead, gently push the nub fiber toward the base yarn as it spins.

Let it do this, using your fingers to form the nub around the yarn, molding it like clay. Make sure the nub fiber is being led in at a 90-degree angle to the base yarn. That's it!

Instructions are excerpted from Handspun Revolution, *by Pluckyfluff.*

Try this technique with different materials for different looks and vary the size of premade sections to make big and small nubs.

For smooth nubs: Use combed rovings.

For lumpy nubs: Use uncarded wool or other fibers

For mixed materials: Try down fibers carded with mohair, yarn scraps, or straight sparkle fibers.

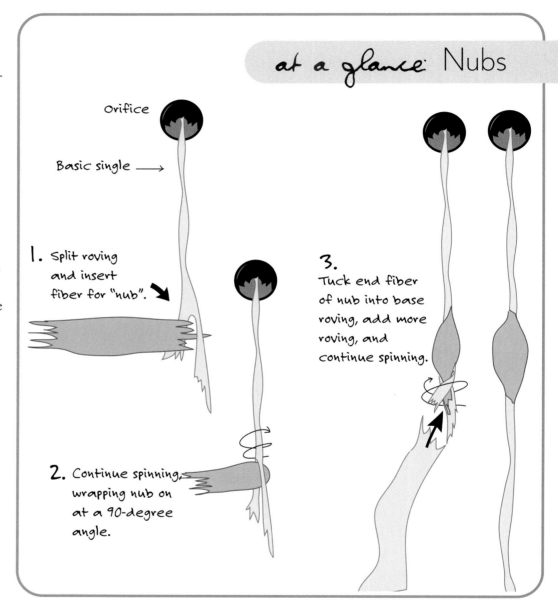

at a glance Nubs

Orifice

Basic single →

1. Split roving and insert fiber for "nub".

2. Continue spinning, wrapping nub on at a 90-degree angle.

3. Tuck end fiber of nub into base roving, add more roving, and continue spinning.

Wool yarn with black nubs and rainbow mohair cocoons

Cocoons

A cocoon is simply a big lofty version of a nub. Use lighter-weight fiber such as carded mohair clouds to create this effect. Follow the basic instructions described previously, only use less tension and allow the fiber to wind on more gently and with some air between the fiber and the core.

Knotty Little Slub yarns by Jenny Neutron Star

Knotty Little Slub

Materials

4 oz (113 g) fiber of choice

Fiber Prep

Any type of fiber can be used for this yarn, although the knotty slub sections require a yarn with longer fibers. They should also be carded so all the fibers line up in the same direction. Cotton, angora, and some sparkle fibers are not good for the knotty slubs. You may also want to consider using a contrasting or different color from that of the base yarn. The fiber you choose for the knotty slubs should be separated into small pieces about 4" (10 cm) long.

Spin!

Using the fiber you selected for the base yarn, spin a single for a few yards (meters). Now stop spinning and take up one of the pieces of the fiber you pre-sized and selected for the knotty slubs. In one hand, hold the base yarn straight out from the

wheel as you normally would. Then take the 4" (10 cm) piece of knotty fiber and hold it at a 90-degree angle from the base yarn. Now begin to spin, continuing to hold the knotty fiber at a 90-degree angle and letting it pile on top of the base yarn. As soon as it starts to pile on, start moving it downward so that it covers about a 2" (5 cm) area. This pile should be thickest at its middle point and should thin out on the edges to blend together with the base yarn. This type of pile is also called a nub (see page 86). Once you have made your slub you can continue spinning the base yarn for about 1" (2.5 cm). Remove any loose fibers from the bottom so that all you see is the newly made slub with 1" (2.5 cm) of base yarn below it and no (or very little) loose roving hanging from the end. Now stop, and tie a knot in the slub. The knot should be made right in the center of the slub and not in any part of the base yarn. You have just made a Knotty Little Slub! Continue to spin the base fiber, pull

the knotty slub through the orifice, and hand wind onto the bobbin. Repeat, adding knotty slubs whenever you like, until the bobbin is full.

Set the Twist

Unwind the yarn from the bobbin and onto a niddy noddy. Prepare a hot water bath. Remove the skein from the niddy noddy and submerge in the water bath. Soak the skein for 20 minutes. Remove from the water and squeeze out any excess water by hand. Place the skein in the washing machine on the spin cycle and spin until all water is removed. Stretch the skein on a tensioner or between some chairs. Use sufficient tension to make the skein taut. Pull all of the knotty slubs to the outside of the skein so that they are not crushed in between the yarn strands. Allow to air-dry completely before removing from tensioner.

Yarn concept and instructions courtesy of Jenny Neutron Star, www.jennyneutronstar.com.

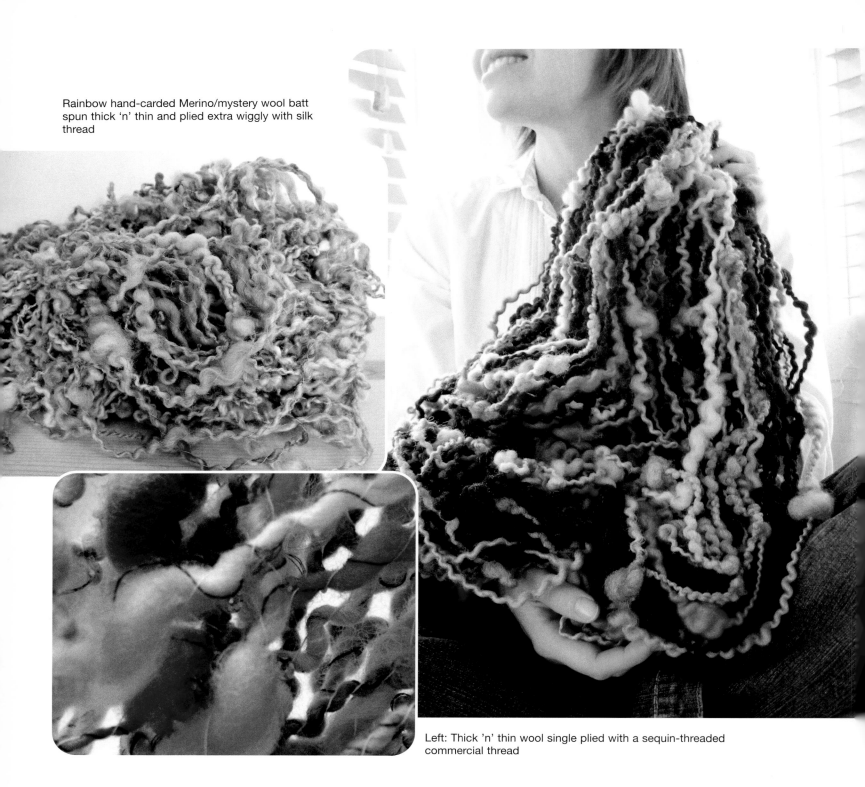

Rainbow hand-carded Merino/mystery wool batt spun thick 'n' thin and plied extra wiggly with silk thread

Left: Thick 'n' thin wool single plied with a sequin-threaded commercial thread

Thread Plying

This technique is technically the same as traditional plying; the only difference is that one ply is substantially thinner than the other. Any fiber can be thread-plied. However, very short fibers are hard to work with (e.g., cotton, downy fibers). Silk, hemp, wool, and alpaca all lend themselves to this technique. However, of all the fibers, dense, spongy wool (minimally processed) usually responds the best. This type of fiber develops more lively coils and waves and ends up with nice buoyancy. Try hand-carded Merino or Dorset for this look.

NOTE: Thick 'n' thin singles will have the most dramatic effect with this technique.

Materials
1 or more bobbin(s) full of pre-spun thick 'n thin single-ply yarn, any fiber
Sewing thread; embroidery thread; or lace-weight yarn

tip: Slightly overspin your singles for the best results (plying tends to take the twist out of the single.)

Thread your single-ply yarn and plying thread through your leader and begin plying normally. (Remember, if you spun your single to the right, you need to ply to the left or vice versa.) In traditional plying, both plys come together at a 45-degree angle, twisting around each other evenly. When thread plying, the idea is to use the thread as a tool to create waves and coils in the single. To do this, the plying thread must always hold the tension while the single should have very little tension.

Ply!
Keep the plying thread directly in line with the orifice (keeping it tensioned at all times) and let the single spin on at a 45-degree angle. Change the angle of the single for different effects:
45-degree angle: gentle wave
90-degree angle: dense coils
100-degree angle: overlapped coils (see Granny Stacks, page 102)

You can keep the angle consistent throughout the plying to make a very consistent, even yarn, or mix up the angle to create a yarn that waves as well as wiggles!

at a glance
Thread Plying

orifice

Keep the tension on the plying thread, not the yarn that is being plied.

45 degrees

Coils

Beehive Coil

Ice-blue merino with beehive coils in solid sparkle fiber

Instructions excerpted from Handspun Revolution *by* Pluckyfluff.

Contrasting Beehive Coil

Materials

4 oz (113 g) wool or other fiber

1 oz (28 g) contrasting fiber (either a different color or a different fiber)
120 yds (110 m) plying thread

Fiber Prep

Start by choosing two wool rovings in contrasting colors. One color will make up the bulk of your yarn while the other will make sporadic spots (beehives) throughout. Prepare the roving for spinning by stripping it apart into manageable pieces. The base color should be in easy-to-spin strips and the contrasting roving should be in pre-drafted sections measuring approximately 1 x 4" (2.5 x 10 cm). (The small sections should end up spinning the same diameter as the base yarn.) A little extra preparation like this will make spinning go much faster!

Spin!

Start spinning your base color roving into a single. Every now and then spin in the small sections of contrasting roving. It is up to you how many of these little sections to add. A few will result in a fairly even material with little beehives popping up here and there, while adding many will result in a very lumpy, bubbly material where the beehive color will tend to dominate.

Once your bobbin is full, replace it with a new one and prepare to ply in the opposite direction from your single. Choose a sturdy sewing thread for plying. I like to use silk thread because it is stronger than cotton and has a nice shine to it.

The plying stage is the most important stage for creating the effect you want in this yarn. Take a little time to imagine what you want this yarn to look like. For the most dramatic effect the base yarn should be plied in a nice gentle wave to contrast with the tightly coiled beehives. To do this, you need to increase the tension so that the bobbin is taking the yarn in fairly fast and not adding a lot of twist (but not so much tension that

at a glance Coils

Orifice

Orifice

Ply gently for several inches (centimeters). Holding the plying thread taut, push the yarn up the thread toward the orifice.

Wraps should stack up against each other, forming coils.

1.

2.

there is no twisting). Use the first few yards (meters) that you spin to make these adjustments until you find a tension that is comfortable and that gives the effect of a wiggly wave rather than a dense twist. It is helpful to hold the thread tighter than the single, allowing the single to gently wrap around the thread.

Now for the beehive!

Ply the yarn in this manner until you get to the first small section of contrasting color. At this point, switch the tension to the single rather than the thread. You will need to anchor the beehive by spinning the thread tightly for several turns at the point where the two colors meet. You

Once you know how to make the simple beehive coil, the super-coil is easy. It is basically one nonstop beehive.

do this by bringing the single directly in front of the orifice (90 degrees) and spinning the thread in *at one point* at a 90-degree angle to the yarn. Two or three turns is plenty to keep the beehive from sliding up.

Return the thread to the straight position and ply the length of the

contrasting color, then stop at the bottom. Pinch the yarn where the two colors meet and push the single up the thread, making coils as it goes up. Keep the yarn pinched so that the twist does not continue down the yarn. Spin another anchor by putting the tension back on the single and feeding the thread in from the side again. Switch the thread back to the main position and continue the gentle plying until you reach the next contrasting section.

Super-Coil
Materials
4oz (113 g) fiber (wool works best)

Spin!
Start by spinning a simple single-ply yarn in one or several colors.

IMPORTANT: Spin this single with a little more twist than you normally would; this will help balance the unwinding that happens when plying the super-coil.

Ply!
Choose a very strong thread, smooth string, or lace-weight yarn for plying (keep it skinny!).

Ply in the opposite direction from the single, keeping the tension on the thread. Do not allow the yarn to wind onto the bobbin. Ply the single for 3" (7.5 cm), then push it up the thread (just like making the beehive). Ply the next 3" (7.5 cm), then push it up the thread so the coils sit right next to the last bunch of coils. Repeat this action for about 12" (30.5 cm) or so, then let the coiled yarn wind onto the bobbin. (If the orifice or your guides are small, you may have to hand wind onto the bobbin a little.) Continue alternating bunching and winding for the entire yarn.

tip: To make a tightly coiled and even yarn-ply for only 2" to 3" (5 to 7.5 cm) before bunching the coils. To make a thick and thin coiled yarn, ply for 6" (15 cm) or so before bunching.

This style combines several other techniques to make a very dramatic yarn. Refer to Nubs, Thread Plying, and Coils for the skills needed to make this yarn.

Crescents

Materials

4 oz (113 g) any fiber
1 oz (28 g) fiber in contrasting color for crescents (wool works best)
Plying thread or lace-weight yarn

Spin!

Spin a single yarn with nubs in a contrasting color (see Nubs, page 87).

Ply!

Ply the single with a thin plying material such as thread or lace-weight yarn (see Thread Plying, page 94). Adjust the tension to medium/high so that the yarn plies in a gentle wave rather than with a lot of twist. Be sure to keep the tension on the plying thread and allow the yarn to wrap around it. When you get to a nub, simply keep the plying thread taut with one hand, and push the nub up the thread toward the orifice until it forms a loop or *crescent* with the other hand. Continue plying. Repeat the process with each nub.

Set the Yarn

Once the bobbin is full, remove the yarn, then soak in hot water for about 20 minutes to set the yarn. Allow to air-dry completely.

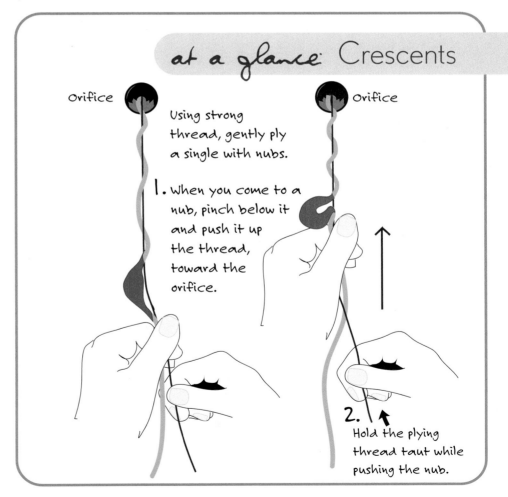

at a glance Crescents

Using strong thread, gently ply a single with nubs.

Orifice

1. When you come to a nub, pinch below it and push it up the thread, toward the orifice.

Orifice

2. Hold the plying thread taut while pushing the nub.

Granny Stacks

This technique is called Granny Stacks because the coils resemble an old-fashioned grandmother hairdo. Picture an old granny on the porch, rolling pin in hand, a delicate layer of flour dusting the stack of intertwined braids and curls on her head. The coils in this yarn are just like those hairstyles; they look good and they're in there tight, but it's hard to figure out just how they got that way.

NOTE: First read Thread Plying, page 94, to get familiar with the function of thread in this technique.

Materials

Bobbin full of pre-spun single ply, any fiber
Plying thread or lace-weight yarn

Ply!

Begin plying, following the instructions for Thread Plying. To make a granny stack, simply hold the plying thread directly in line with the orifice (keeping full tension on the thread), then hold the single-ply yarn out at a

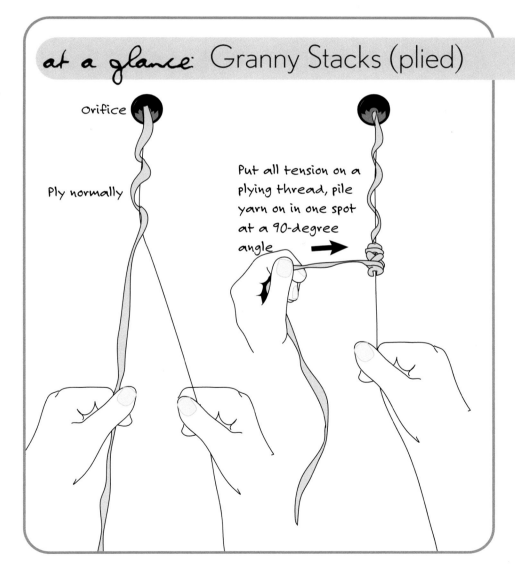

at a glance: Granny Stacks (plied)

Orifice

Ply normally

Put all tension on a plying thread, pile yarn on in one spot at a 90-degree angle →

Hand-dyed and carded Merino plied into giant stacks on a pom-pom thread.
This variation of the technique is included here courtesy of Mirror Mirror.

90-degree angle and allow it to wind onto the thread *in one place*. Once it has begun to wind itself around the plying thread, move the single up even more toward the wheel (another 10 degrees or so). The yarn will begin to backtrack on itself, creating a coil that winds toward the orifice. Work 1" (2.5 cm), then bring the single back down to the 90-degree position. If the stack is as big as you want it, simply bring the single down to the 45-degree position and continue plying normally.

Most granny stacks will need to be fished through the orifice with the threading hook and hand wound onto the bobbin.

NOTE: See the PluckyFluff Advice Center, page 145, for information about how to draw big elements through the orifice.

Crazy Granny

For giant crazy-granny stacks, follow the instructions described previously, except backtrack further toward the orifice and then back over the stack moving toward you, covering a 3 – 4" (7.5 – 10 cm) space overall. Continue plying the stack on in this zone, moving the single back and forward many times, to create a giant stack.

Crazy grannies work best with a thin overspun single. The extra twist in the single will ensure that the yarn does not become unspun and weak during the plying process.

This technique should be done on a wheel with a large orifice, measuring at least ½" (1.3 cm) in diameter.

Single Granny

This is a granny stack made on a single-ply yarn rather than a plied yarn.

Materials

4 oz (113 g) roving
100 yds (91.5 m) core thread

Begin spinning a basic single with a core thread. You can spin the core thread on the inside or candy-stripe it around the outside.

Make a stack!

Hold the core thread out of the way (at a 90-degree angle) and spin the next few inches (centimeters) of yarn. Make sure the core thread does not get spun down the yarn. It should wrap around the yarn in one spot, making a little bead.

Now reverse the positions, bringing the core thread down directly in front of the orifice and holding the single out at a 90-degree angle. Allow the single to wrap on from the side in one spot, forming a stack.

Once the stack is complete, bring the roving and the thread back together and continue spinning normally.

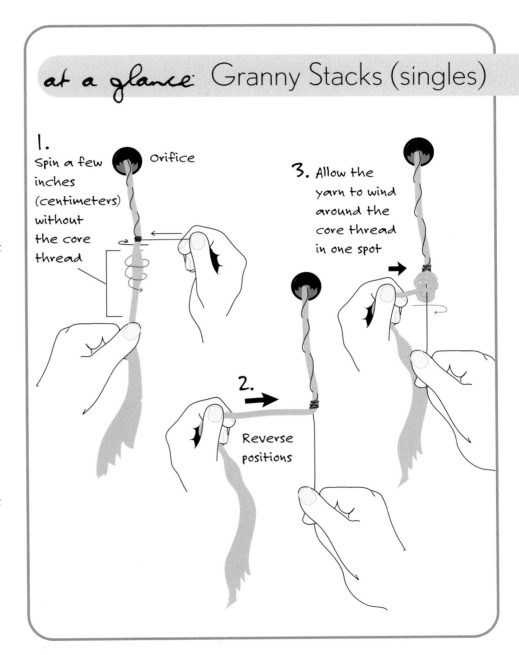

at a glance: Granny Stacks (singles)

1. Spin a few inches (centimeters) without the core thread
Orifice

2. Reverse positions

3. Allow the yarn to wind around the core thread in one spot

Lavender merino
carded with black
silk noil spun thick
'n' thin and plied
with silk thread by
Pluckyfluff

Twists

Materials

4 oz (113 g) fiber of choice
100 yds (91.5 cm) plying thread

Wool works best for this technique, but almost any fiber can be made to work. Use a fiber that has a lot of memory and tends to hold its twist. These twists can also be added strategically. For example, you can spin a yarn with mohair and every now and then add a 3 – 4" (7.5 – 10 cm) section of wool. When you go to ply the yarns, the wool will twist but the mohair will stay relatively straight. You can do this with wool and silk, wool and hemp, wool and cotton, and so forth. In an all-wool yarn it will be the thin sections that make the twists and the thick sections that remain straight. So if you are going to use 100 percent wool you *must* spin it thick and thin! The following instructions are for an all-wool yarn.

Fiber Prep

Select some wool for the yarn. Hand-carded or lightly processed wool is best as it retains the most energy and loft. Super-wash, combed top, and other over-processed wools can be pretty dead and will require a lot more twist to get the life back into them.

Next, decide how you want this yarn to look. If you want the twists to be subtle, then choose one color scheme for the entire yarn. However, if you want the twists to contrast, then choose a specific color just for the twists. Break the "twists" roving into small pieces, just enough to spin into 3 – 4" (7.5 – 10 cm) long sections. Prepare the remaining wool by splitting it into easy to spin sections.

Spin!

Begin spinning a simple single. Be sure to spin a thick 'n' thin yarn. An evenly spun yarn will not twist as easily! If spinning a single color scheme, simply spin through the fiber. If making contrasting twists, spin the base color every few yards (2-3 meters), or as often as you like, then stop and spin in a small 3 – 4" (7.5 – 10 cm) section in the contrasting color. Spin through the fiber, then remove the bobbin and prepare to ply.

Ply!

Select a delicate yet strong thread to ply with. Attach your wool single and plying thread to the leader string and begin to spin *in the opposite direction* that you spun the single in. *Keep more tension on the thread*, less on the single. Keep the thread directly in front of you and let the single wind on at a 45-degree angle. Ply like this for a few yards (meters). If you are spinning a solid color, simply watch the single as it approaches your hands. It will have spots where it is naturally twisted. Take advantage of these places. As the twist approaches, grab it with one hand, pinching the

---

This technique is courtesy of Jenny Neutron Star. It is one of my favorites and bound to become one of yours.

base of the twist so it does not straighten out. With the other hand, guide the ply down to the upcoming twist. Ply right up to the base of the twist, keeping it pinched the whole time. Tightly ply past the base of the twist and on through the single. Repeat for every twist that approaches.

For contrasting twists, work this process for every "twist color" section that approaches. If the section does not want to twist naturally, simply twist it by hand and follow the steps described previously.

Set the Twist

Unwind the bobbin onto a niddy noddy. Make a hot water bath and remove the skein from the niddy noddy. Soak the skein for 10-20 minutes. Place the skein in the washing machine, set on the spin cycle, and spin to remove excess water. Hang the skein to dry.

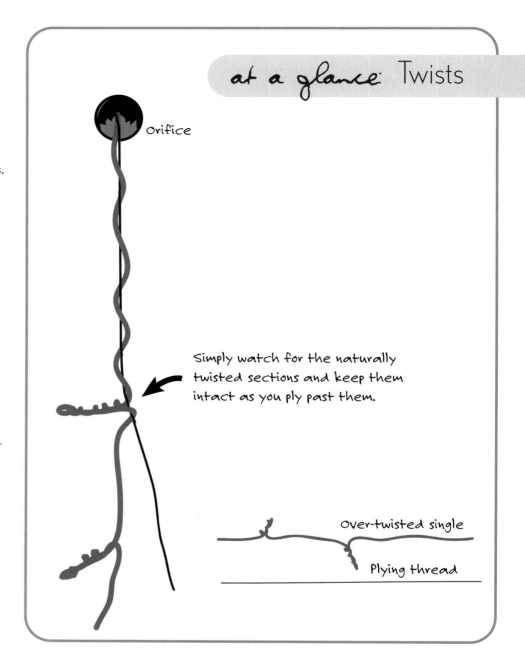

at a glance: Twists

Orifice

Simply watch for the naturally twisted sections and keep them intact as you ply past them.

Over-twisted single

Plying thread

Twists in Singles

Materials

4 oz (113 g) fiber of choice
Core thread (silk embroidery thread
works great)

Begin spinning a simple single along with a core thread (or candy-striped). When you are ready to spin a twist, simply hold the core thread out at a 90-degree angle, keeping it from twisting along the yarn, and spin the next few inches (centimeters) of fiber *without a core thread in it*. The core thread will wrap around the yarn in one spot a few times, but this is okay.

Stop the wheel and pinch the core thread where it is attached to the yarn. Allow the few inches (centimeters) you just spun without the core thread to wrap up in a twist. Pinch the base of this twist to the spot where the core thread is attached and continue spinning. The core thread should get caught up in the roving and continue spinning a normal single.

Soak and set this yarn.

An example of twists in singles. The yellow section above the twist is actually the core thread where it twisted in place while I spun the *twist* section. It creates the effect of a band or bead. *Note:* The feathered look is from unspun hemp fiber

This is a *twist* on Twists, worked in a single-ply yarn with a core thread.

Felt Add-Ins

Create felt embellishments for your yarn using your favorite felting technique. Try needle felting for detailed objects or try my favorite method: roll bits of wool into balls between your palms, stick them in a sock, knot the sock at the end, and throw the whole kit and caboodle in the washing machine on the HOT cycle. Run the machine for one or two cycles and you've got sweet little felt bobbles.

NOTE: Be sure to make the felt objects small enough to fit through the orifice of your wheel.

Materials

4 oz (113 g) fiber for base yarn (your choice)
10 -15 felt objects
½ oz (14 g) combed fiber for threading
Large quilting or darning needle (sharp)

Prepare Felt Objects

Tear off 10–15 small strips about 2 x ½" (5 x 1.3 cm) from a combed-top roving or other smooth fiber. Twist the tail ends of this fiber tightly and form a little loop that can be easily threaded through your needle. Pull

tip: Thread the roving *opposite* the most attractive side of the felt object. This will ensure that the best view will face out in the final material.

Felt maki sushi courtesy of Jungle
www.jungle.etsy.com

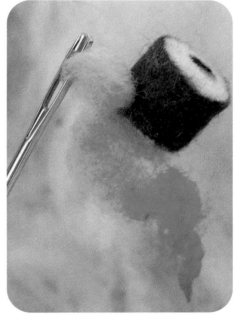

Threading roving through felt maki.

1" (2.5 cm) or so through the eye of your needle. Using this needle, thread the roving through the felt object. Repeat the process until all felt the objects are threaded.

Spin!

Begin spinning a simple single with the fiber of your choice. Spin a few yards (meters), then stop the wheel and break off the roving, leaving only a few inches (centimeters) unspun. Tease the roving out a little where the twist hits the unspun fiber. Grab a felt object and lay the tail end of the threaded roving into this spot. Pinch the add-in roving to the base yarn roving and begin spinning, making

sure the two rovings are twisting together securely. Spin up to and beyond the felt object, guiding the two rovings together the whole way. Make sure the tail end of the add-in roving tucks neatly into the base yarn. Tack on more base yarn fiber and continue spinning normally. Repeat this process periodically, throughout the length of the yarn.

tip: Make sure you put plenty of twist in the yarn around the felt add-ins to ensure that they sit securely in the base yarn.

Set the Twist

Transfer the finished yarn from your bobbin to your niddy noddy, keeping tension on the yarn *the whole time.* Prepare a bath of very hot water. Submerge the skein completely and

let soak for 10 to 15 minutes. Remove from the water and place the skein in the washing machine on the spin cycle to remove any excess water. Immediately transfer the yarn to a tensioner, set the tensioner very tight, and allow the skein to completely air-dry before removing.

tip: Use this technique to add any soft item to your yarns; if you can thread it—you can add it!

Hat crocheted from felt add-in yarn by Cindy Cole

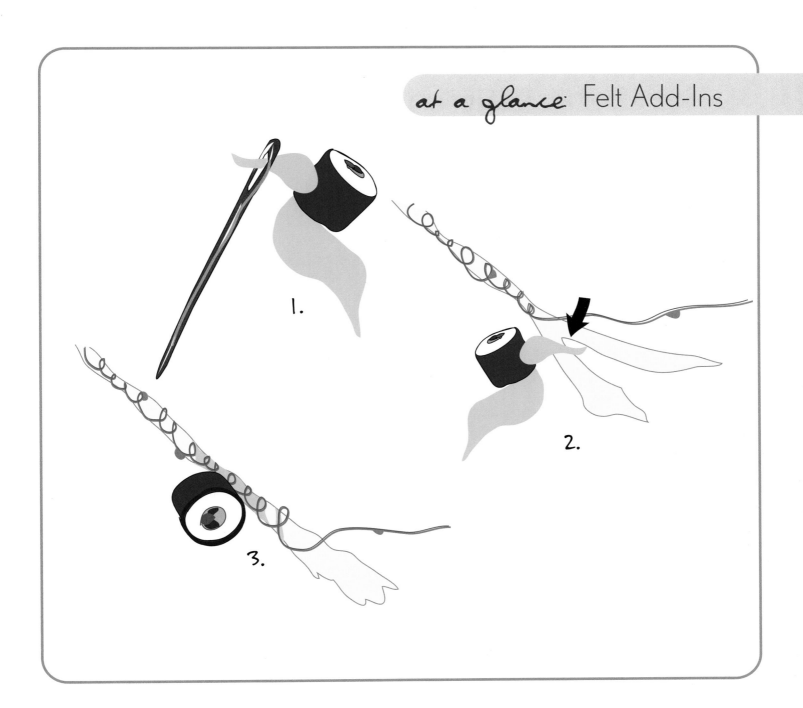

1.

2.

3.

Semi-Felted Bubbles

Materials

4 oz (113 g) wool batts or roving
½- 1 oz (14 – 28 g) semi-felted wool

Those little clumps of felted wool at the bottom of your fiber stash are a fiber dream come true: textured, bubbly, full of character, and best of all, easy to spin. So save them up—it's time to spin your next favorite yarn.

Fiber Prep

Wool works best for this yarn because it will naturally grab onto the fiber bubbles. Smooth fibers such as silk will tend to slip off, and short fibers like cotton won't hold enough twist. Select some wool roving or a carded wool-base batt and lay it out on your workspace in easy-to-spin sections, ready to go.

Semi-Felted Bubbles

You can add a few of these to a yarn for a little dimension or add a lot for a dynamic high-texture yarn. Collect your semi-felted wool and nicest looking parts; attractively shaped bubbles, good color combinations, etc., then tear these pieces off from the main clump. A good spinnable size should fit through the orifice easily. It is possible to spin bigger pieces, but they will have to be worked through the orifice carefully by hand (see the Pluckyfluff Advice Center, page 145). Do not cut the bubbles off with scissors! Fibers need naturally tapered ends in order to cling together and using scissors will leave blunt ends. Tear the fiber for best results. Once you have enough semi-felted bits, go through each one and draft out the fibers on each end, making tails that will attach easily to the base yarn.

Spin!

Using your base yarn fiber, spin a few yards (meters) in a simple single, then stop the wheel and break off the base roving, leaving only a few unspun inches (centimeters). Split this roving in half. Pick up a semi-felted wool bubble and lay one of the drafted tail ends into the split. Pinching the fibers together with one hand, begin spinning again. Keep the fibers pinched together as the twist travels through the bubble, joining the bubble to the base. STOP, split the roving again, and tuck the remaining tail end of the bubble into the base fiber, pinching it together. Resume spinning, trapping the last of the bubble fibers between the base fibers to form a solid yarn. Reconnect the base roving and continue spinning. Repeat process throughout the yarn.

Set the Twist

It is important to soak and set the twist on this yarn. Follow the "Set the Twist" instructions on page 83. Pull the skein tight enough to have tension on all the bubbles. While the skein is still damp, go through and pull all the bubbles to the outside of the skein. Make sure each one retains its shape and is not smashed between the yarn strands. Allow to air dry completely.

Bow Ties and Butterflies

Materials

4 oz (113 g) base fiber
2+ yds (1.8+ m) seam binding or ribbon
100 yds (91.5 m) core thread

Fiber Prep

Lay out a selection of fiber(s) for your base yarn. Separate into manageable sections. Longer fibers will hold the bow ties more securely, but as long as you have a core thread shorter fibers will also work.

Bow Ties

Select a 3 to 4 yards (2.7 to 3.6 m) of seam binding or silk ribbon and cut into 2" (5 cm) sections. The ends can be cut blunt or at an angle, whichever look you prefer.

Butterflies

For butterflies, use lacy or gauzy material and cut larger rectangles, about 1" x 2½" (2.5 x 6.5 cm)

Core Thread

Select a thread that that is strong but not bulky. If you want to spin it on the outside (candy-striping method), choose something that will complement your other materials. If you spin it on the inside, it doesn't matter what it looks like as long as it's sturdy. Silk thread is one of the strongest threads, and it's pretty, too!

Spin!

Connect the core thread and base roving to the leader string and begin spinning normally. Spin 3 to 4 yards (2.7 to 3.6 m), then stop the wheel and break off the base roving, leaving only a few unspun inches. Pick up a bowtie or butterfly and lay it flat between the base roving and the core thread. It should lay *perpendicular* to the base yarn. Pinch the fabric/ribbon between the core thread and roving with one hand and start the wheel spinning again. Spin up to and *just*

past the ribbon/fabric, making sure that the ends of the ribbon remain sticking out. Spin *just past* the ribbon/fabric and STOP.

Keep the roving pinched together at the base of the ribbon/fabric, then use your other hand to pull the core thread firmly toward you. Give the core thread a little tug; this should pinch the center of the ribbon, creating a bow-tie shape. If it doesn't, then you have spun too far past the ribbon for the technique to work. Try it again with the next one, making sure

there are only one or two twists beyond the ribbon. Once you've mastered the technique, reconnect your base roving and continue spinning. Repeat the process, adding a butterfly or bow tie every few yards (meters). Add them more often for a dense look or less often for a quilty, more sporadic look.

Set the Twist

It is imperative to set the twist on this yarn. Unwind the yarn from the bobbin and onto a niddy noddy. Prepare a hot water bath. Remove the skein from the noddy and submerge it in the water bath. Let the skein soak for about 20 minutes. Remove the skein and hand squeeze out excess water. Put the skein in the washing machine on the spin cycle until all water is removed. Stretch the skein on a tensioner or between some chairs. Pull the skein tight enough to have tension on all the bow ties. While the skein is still damp, go through and pull all the bow ties to the outside of the skein. Make sure each one is flat and open, and not tangled or caught between the yarn. Let dry.

Pinch just below the ribbon and put a few tight twists in.

Give the thread a good tug to make the bow tie shape.

Pom-poms made from Jute twine, spun onto a wool base yarn

Tufts and Pom-poms

Materials

4 oz (113 g) wool or other base fiber of choice

20+ yds (18 m) miscellaneous yarns, threads, string, etc.

100 yds (91.5 m) sturdy core thread

NOTE: See Candy Striping, page 72, for use of the core thread.

Fiber Prep

Prepare a base fiber for your yarn. Any wool roving or batt will work, as well as other medium-long fibers (hemp, silk, etc). Cotton fibers are too short to use for this technique.

Tufts

Select a yarn or a mix of yarns and threads to make the tufts. This is a great technique for those odds and ends left over from old projects. Lay the balls of yarns and spools of thread around you on the floor, each in its own bucket or bowl. Collect all the loose ends from the balls and tie them together. Using your niddy noddy, begin to wrap the collection of strings into a skein. Make enough wraps so the skein is about 2" (5 cm) wide. When you have enough yarns wrapped on the niddy noddy, use scissors to cut the yarns/strings free from the balls on the floor. Pull the newly formed skein off the niddy noddy, and hold the skein in one spot so it does not get tangled. Cut evenly through the loop near the tag ends. The yarns should now be in a long ponytail. Lay this ponytail over a flat surface and begin to cut through it at 3" (7.5 cm) intervals. Make neat, even stacks of the newly cut sections, ready for use.

Pom-Poms

Using the same technique described previously, prepare neat stacks of cut

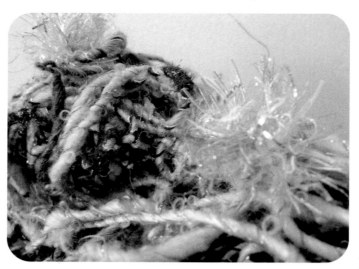

yarns. Choose one of the threads or yarns from your selection and cut 6" (15 cm) lengths. Grab a small bunch of cut yarn sections; a few will make a sparse pom-pom, and more lengths will make a bushy one. Lay the stack of yarns *perpendicular* across the 6" (15 cm) length of yarn/thread. Bring both ends of the 6" (15 cm) yarn/thread up and around the center of the stack. Cinch it down very tight and tie off in a square knot. Holding both ends of the thread/yarn in one hand, use your other hand to fluff the pom-pom. These pom-poms are the same as those traditionally used on hats.

NOTE: Make sure the thread/yarn ends used to cinch the pom-pom remain separated. These ends will be used to spin the pom-pom onto the yarn.

Core thread

Select a fairly strong thread to spin along with this yarn. It is necessary to tack the tufts in tightly. Choose something that looks good with your other materials, because it will show in the yarn.

Spin!

Attach the core thread and base roving to your leader string and begin spinning a simple single. You can spin the roving around the core thread or have the core thread wrap around the outside of the yarn (see Candy Striping, page 72), whichever is most comfortable. After a few yards (meters), stop spinning and break off the roving, leaving only a few unspun inches (centimeters). Split this tail end of roving in half, with the core thread tucked into one of the halves. From your stacks of cut yarn, grab a small pinch of yarns/threads. Lay this group of cut yarn lengths into the split in the roving. They should lay perpendicular to the direction of the roving and core thread, forming a plus sign. Sandwich the bunch of yarns between the roving and pinch it tightly back together.

Tufts

Keeping the roving pinched together behind the bunch of yarns, start the wheel spinning again. The twist should run through the stack and beyond, securing it in the yarn. Pull the core thread firmly toward you as the tuft is spun in. This will ensure that there is a tight wrap around the tuft. Spin a few inches (centimeters) beyond the tuft. Reconnect your base roving and continue spinning. Pull the tuft through the orifice (see the Pluckyfluff Advice Center, page 145) and hand wind onto the bobbin. Repeat the process every few yards (meters).

Pom-Poms

Attach the core thread and base roving to your leader string and begin spinning a simple single. You can spin the roving around the core thread or have the core thread wrap around the outside of the yarn (see Candy Striping, page 72), whichever is most comfortable. Spin a few yards (meters), then stop the wheel and select a pom-pom. Choose one of the loose tag ends of the thread/yarn used to cinch the pom-pom and tuck it into the roving that you are working with in the spinning zone. Continue spinning, making sure that the cinch thread gets trapped inside the twisting roving. Spin up to the pom-pom.

Split the roving underneath the pom-pom and insert the remaining tag end of thread. Continue spinning, making sure the tag end is spun tightly into the base yarn. The two tag ends should serve as anchors, one leading up to the pom-pom and the other leading away.

Set the Twist

It is imperative to set the twist on this yarn. Unwind the yarn from the bobbin and onto a niddy noddy. Prepare a hot water bath. Remove the skein from the noddy and submerge the skein in the water bath. Soak the skein for 20 minutes. Remove and squeeze out excess water by hand. Place the skein in washing machine, set on the spin cycle, and spin the skein until all water is removed. Stretch the skein on a tensioner or between some chairs. Pull the skein tight enough to have tension on all the pom-poms. While the skein is still damp, locate all the tufts/pom-poms and hand fluff them up so they don't dry crumpled.

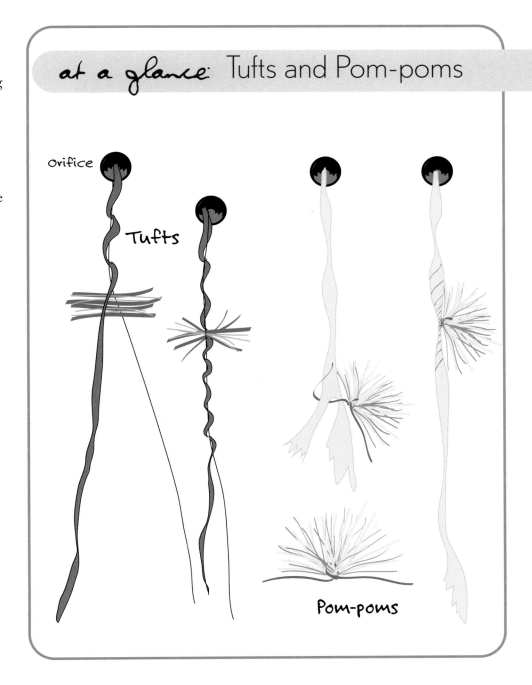

at a glance Tufts and Pom-poms

Orifice

Tufts

Pom-poms

Silkworm cocoons spun into wool with black plastic spike novelty thread and felt balls

Silkworm

Both silkworm cocoons and carrier rods can be purchased readily on the Internet; simply search by those terms. They are relatively inexpensive and almost always come washed and undyed. The cocoons come whole or with a hole cut in them. The hole is where the cocoon was opened to remove the silkworm before the silk was harvested. These cocoons are quite strong and you will need a good heavy-duty darning needle to poke through them. These can be spun easily into a single-ply yarn, either plain or with a striping thread (see Candy Striping, page 72). A singles yarn with cocoons spun in *cannot be plied*, as plying will undo the twist that is holding them in place.

Cocoons
10–12 silkworm cocoons
4 oz (113 g) any wool fiber

Dye!
Silkworm cocoons take dyes very well. You can use both wool dyes and plant dyes. Follow the directions on your dye package and dye the cocoons just as you would any other fiber. Drain off excess water and let the cocoons to dry.

tip: The cocoons will be slightly softer when wet, so it may be a bit easier to thread them before they are completely dry.

Thread the cocoons
Take a small amount, about ½" x 2" (1.3 x 5 cm), of the fiber you intend to make the yarn from, and twist the end into a point. Thread this through the eye of the needle. Wearing a thimble, (I have impaled myself more times threading cocoons than any other material!) thread the fiber through the cocoon. Don't insert the needle straight through the middle, but rather go through a corner of the cocoon. Enter and exit as if you are just making a small stitch. If you are using the open cocoons, thread through the opposite end from the hole. This will ensure that the hole faces out when you spin it into the yarn.

Spin!
On a quill or wheel with a very large orifice, begin spinning a basic single. When you are ready to add a cocoon, simply stop the wheel, split the roving, and lay the threaded fiber on your cocoon in the gap in the roving. Pinch the fibers together and spin up to the cocoon. Stop, tuck the tail end of the cocoon's fiber into the roving, and continue spinning behind the cocoon. The fiber that runs through the cocoon should be tightly spun into the yarn both in front of and behind the cocoon.

Continue spinning and adding cocoons until the bobbin is full. Remove the yarn, soak in hot water for 10 minutes, spin out excess water, and let allow the yarn to dry on a stretcher.

Hand-dyed silk carrier rods

Silk Carrier Rod Yarn

These silk carrier rods need to be spun while they are wet. So prepare your spinning fiber, wheel, and anything else you might need while the rods are dyeing. If the rods are already dyed, soak them in a warm water bath for 10 minutes, then spin off the extra water in the washing machine before proceeding. This yarn requires a thread for structure, either core spun or candy-striped (see Candy Striping, page 72).

Materials

10–12 dyed silk carrier rods
4 oz (113 g) any fiber
Core thread or lace-weight yarn

Dye!

Dye the carrier rods according to the instructions on your wool or plant dyes. Drain the rods and place in the washing machine set on the spin cycle to extract excess water.

Prepare the rods

While the rods are still wet, draft the ends out to form long spinnable strands that can be used to spin into the yarn. They will not draft perfectly and may tear into flaps and chunks, but the main idea here is to make the ends skinny and ragged enough to readily catch hold in the roving as you spin it.

Spin!

Begin spinning a basic single with either a core thread or a striping thread (it does not make a difference for function whether the thread is spun inside or outside the yarn). When you are ready to add a carrier rod, stop the wheel and break off the roving (leave the core thread remains attached), leaving 2 – 3" (5–7.5 cm) inches of unspun fiber. Split this fiber in two and sandwich the ragged end of a carrier rod between the roving. Pinch the roving, thread an end of the carrier rod together, and continue spinning, allowing the twist to catch all three and twist them together.

Now for the tricky part! Once the end of the carrier rod is attached, hold the core thread tight between you and the orifice. Continue spinning and allow the rod to wrap around the core thread at a 45-degree angle. It is similar to twisting paper. Once it has twisted almost to the end, tack on some roving and twist the ragged end of the rod into the roving along with the thread. The rod should be anchored at each end with a little extra twist. Continue until all rods are spun in.

Remove the yarn, soak in hot water for 10 minutes, spin out any excess water, and set the twist on a stretcher.

NOTE: When knitting or crocheting this yarn, you can soak each carrier rod separately and reshape it to suit your design. Simply keep a cup of hot water nearby as you work and soak the carrier rod until it becomes pliable.

Antoinette handspun vintage embroidered fabric with felt beads by Pluckyfluff

Spinning Fabric

This is a great technique for recycling material and saving some money. You may get tired of the style of your clothes, but still love the fabric. So instead of tossing it ... spin it! This style of yarn also looks great when made with vintage fabrics, lace, and old needlework pieces.

Materials

Fabric of choice
2 oz (56.5 g) wool
100 yds (91.5 m) core thread

Fabric Prep

Cut the strips strategically to keep any interesting or embroidered elements intact.

Cut or tear the fabric into 1" (2.5 cm) wide strips (or narrower if you prefer). Look out for interesting characteristics in the fabric and try to keep them intact. Elements such as embroidered flowers, snaps, and stitching can be spun so that they show on the outside of the yarn.

Spin!

Begin by spinning a simple single in wool with a core thread. When you are ready to add the fabric, stop spinning, break off the roving, leaving about 2" (5 cm) unspun. Split this roving in half and insert one end of a fabric strip between the two pieces of roving. Pinch the fabric, roving, and core thread together and resume spinning. The fabric should get trapped and twisted inside the wool. Continue spinning the fabric and core thread *without* any wool roving. Think of the wool as glue and use it to fuse the ends of the fabric strips together. For each connection, use 3 – 4" (7.5 – 10 cm) of roving and overlap it with the two strips and core thread.

For an extra tight connection, you can split each strip at the ends to make a more interlaced binding.

Chenille

Materials

Chenille fabric, arranged in stripes, not dots or floral

4 oz (113 g) wool

Preparation

Using good sharp fabric scissors, cut the chenille fabric into strips. (Cut parallel to the raised chenille.) The strips can be anywhere from 4–24" (10–61 cm) depending on the look you want. Short strips will create small patches in a knit material, whereas long strips will result in a striping effect.

Spin!

Begin spinning a basic single. When you are ready to add the chenille, stop the wheel and break off the wool roving, leaving a couple of inches (centimeters) of unspun fiber. Split the fiber in two and insert the end of a chenille strip into it. Once the che-

nille is trapped between the wool, continue spinning, making sure that the chenille is twisted tightly into the wool. As you spin through the chenille, make sure that it is twisting with the fuzzy side out. If the fuzzy chenille is on the inside, simply flip the strip over. Spin very slowly at first until you are familiar with how the chenille strips behave.

As you near the end of the strip (2-3" (5 to 7.5 cm) from the end, lay some wool roving alongside the strip and allow the twist to join them. Split the wool roving and tuck the last ½" (1.3 cm) of chenille into it and seal it together in the twist. Continue spinning in the wool. Repeat when you are ready for another chenille section.

When the bobbin is full, remove the yarn and soak in hot water for 20 minutes. Spin out excess water and dry on a stretcher.

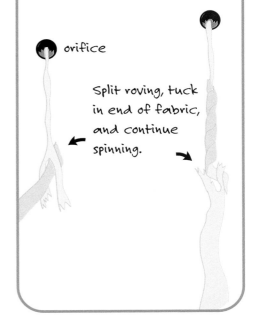

at a glance
Chenille Fabric and Roving

orifice

Split roving, tuck in end of fabric, and continue spinning.

Light green embroidered
Easter dress spun with
red and green Lincoln
locks by Pluckyfluff

Spiral-Cut Dress

Don't throw away that old dress! Give it a new life with this recycled material project. Dresses with interesting accents such as embroidery, lace, and trims will give this yarn extra beauty and texture.

Materials

Second-hand dress
Good sharp scissors
1-2 ozs (28 – 56.5 g) wool or mohair locks
     (or any fibers)

Preparation

Starting at the bottom hem of the dress, begin cutting a ½" (1.3 cm) strip running along the seam. Continue this cut, spiraling all the way up the entire length of the dress. Wind the strip into a ball as you go. Try to preserve as many elements as will fit through the orifice (buttons, snaps, hooks, etc.). If you have to break the strip due to a roadblock (a zipper, for example), simply reconnect the strip with a square knot. The little ends will blend into the yarn and even add character.

Spin!

Pulling from your ball of fabric strip, attach the strip to the leader string on your wheel. Make sure the tension is set fairly high. Begin spinning normally. The tension should be tight enough to pull the fabric yarn through the orifice without overtwisting. Spin through your entire ball of fabric.

Wind the yarn onto a niddy noddy and tie off. Soak the yarn and set.

NOTE: Depending on the material of the dress, soaking and setting may not truly set the twist. For storage, twist into a skein in the opposite direction of its natural twist, or wind into a ball.

tip: For added interest, add uncarded wool locks, roving, or other fiber while spinning just as you would any other material.

This style of yarn is a perfect way to make dramatic trims and edgings. Look for lustrous, long, uncarded wool locks. Lincoln is one of the best breeds for these locks, but you can use any number of other types, such as Icelandic wool or mohair. This yarn can vary from a thick clumpy yarn to an elegant boa, depending on which type of locks you use. For core material, choose something strong and with some grab, such as a commercial mohair yarn.

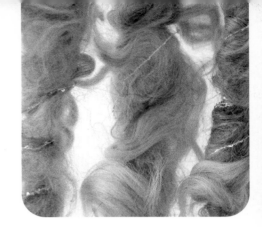

Extreme Tail Spin

Materials

*4 oz (113 g) uncarded long staple locks
such as Lincoln*
Sturdy core material

Fiber Prep

Separate locks into 1 to 3" (2.5 to 7.5 cm) clumps. Identify the base and the tip of each clump and arrange them so all of the locks are orientated in the same direction. You will be spinning the *base* of the locks onto the core thread.

Spin!

Thread the core material through the leader string and, using regular wool roving, spin a simple single for 10–12" (25.5 – 30.5 cm). Begin adding the uncarded locks. Using one or two locks at a time, lay the base of the locks (the end that was sheared, not the narrow tip) against the core thread at a 90-degree angle. Spin, using your thumb and forefinger to pinch and guide the base fiber of the lock as it twists onto the core material. Spin slowly and be sure to

Extreme tailspun yarn crocheted into a bear hat

attach only the base of the lock, allowing the tips to hang free. Once that lock is attached, stop the wheel and, keeping the base of that lock pinched, grab the next uncarded lock and repeat.

This process is a very slow one. You will be starting and stopping every couple of inches (centimeters). Proceed until all the fiber is spun or

until the bobbin is full. After the final lock is attached, tack on some wool roving and spin 10 -12" (25.5 – 30.5 cm) as a simple single the same as the beginning (to be used for tying off the skein).

Unwind onto a niddy noddy, using the spun-single sections to tie off. A full bobbin may only provide you with 3-4 yards (2.75 – 3. 65 meters) of yarn.

at a glance: Extreme Tail Spin

large Orifice →

Attach individual locks to the core thread by pinching the base end of the lock against the thread. Spin until the twist grabs the lock and wraps it around the core. Repeat with each lock.

La Lana Wools, Tailspun Yarns

This style of tailspun and thickspun yarns was pioneered in the late 1970s by Luisa Gelenter, owner and founder of La Lana Wools in Taos, New Mexico. She felt the natural fiber looked most beautiful on the back of the animal. Her desire to recreate this resulted in her Handspun Textured Yarn lines.

During her travels in Bolivia, Luisa sat with the women in the marketplace and learned to handspin Alpaca on a drop spindle. When the time came to dye her handspun yarns, she decided they deserved more than a pinch of powder.

"The dye was cast" so to speak, and so began Luisa's great handspinning adventure. Since then, to honor the craft of spinning, Luisa uses only the finest fibers and still considers natural plant dyes the most beautiful. Luisa's dyeing philosophy is to prepare the fibers and dyes to the best of her ability and let serendipity take over. She is also a big fan of random factors and textures. These interests are evident in the uniqueness of La Lana yarns.

NOTE: Only Luisa and a few close spinners know her special technique for making the dramatic La Lana tailspun yarns. The instructions presented in this book are presented by the author and do not reflect the exact techniques of La Lana Wools.

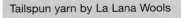

Tailspun yarn by La Lana Wools

Translucent Mohair

Materials

2 oz (56.5 g) mohair clouds (see Resources, page 300)

100 yds (91.5 m) novelty thread or lace weight yarn

¼ oz (7 g) sparkle (optional)

Fiber Prep

The key to achieving this look is to start with the right mohair. Do not use fine-combed, densely packed mohair

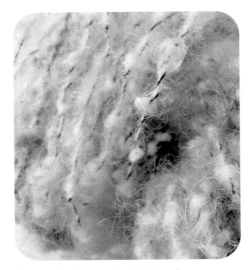

Core spinning on novelty thread

roving. The roving should either be in cloud form (light, airy rolags or hand/drum-carded batts). The mohair should be light, fluffy, and translucent.

Carding

Lay the mohair out in a thin layer on the bed of the drum carder or hand carders. On top of the mohair make another thin layer of sparkle and little bits of colorful wool or other fiber. Place another layer of mohair on top of this, sandwiching the sparkle in between the mohair. Run this through the carder (or hand carders). Repeat the process with the remaining materials.

Core Thread

Choose a thread or lace-weight yarn that will look interesting when seen through the mohair. Pom-poms, bright colors, or metallic threads or fibers work very well, but almost any novelty thread or lace-weight yarn will be attractive.

 Beginners should choose a core thread with a rough texture so that the mohair will grab on more readily.

SPIN!

Attach the core thread and some mohair to the leader string on your bobbin. Begin spinning as you would normally to get the wheel started. Spin a yard (meter) to make sure everything is working properly. Once the yarn is on the bobbin, reduce the tension until there is very little pull into the orifice. If your tension is too tight, it will pull the yarn out of your hand before you can get it fluffy enough.

Fluff the mohair!

 Work with manageable amounts of fiber. Hand-size pieces from the batt are ideal for this technique.

While spinning, hold the core thread and *a small amount of mohair* in one hand and use your other hand to tease the majority of the mohair out and pile it back on itself. As the core thread twists, it will grab onto the very loose mohair fibers. Let the fibers twist around the core just enough to coat it very lightly. If it starts to twist too densely, tease the fiber back out in that spot. The hand-work here is tricky; one hand should always hold the core thread, but it takes *both* hands to simultaneously tease the fiber around the core.

As soon as the mohair is laid on in a sheer wrap, allow that section to wind onto the bobbin. Repeat this process with the remainder of your fiber.

tip: Don't wait for the core thread to pull the mohair on, as the twist is too delicate to detect. Instead, push the mohair onto the core as it's twisting.

Set the twist

This yarn should be pretty balanced without being set, but it is still a good idea to make it perfectly straight. Soak the skein in hot water for 3-5 minutes. Transfer to the washing machine, set the machine on the spin cycle, and spin until excess water is removed. Remove the skein and give it a good shake to fluff out the fibers. Hang or lay flat to dry with *no* tension. The yarn will lose its loftiness if you stretch it during the drying process. This yarn should virtually float when it's dry!

NOTE: If you're a beginner, your first attempts at this technique may yield an over-twisted yarn. If so, you will need to put more tension on your skein while it dries. Use a yarn tensioner, or strand the skein between two chairs.

Orifice

Gently tease the mohair into a fluffy wrap as the core thread is spinning.

Above: *Coral 2007,* Wood-fired porcelain with hand-dyed and spun mohair and merino knitted and felted. Britta Cruz, www.dreamlandart.com

Right: Fiber landscape by Melissa Baker, www.moustacheridesyarn.com

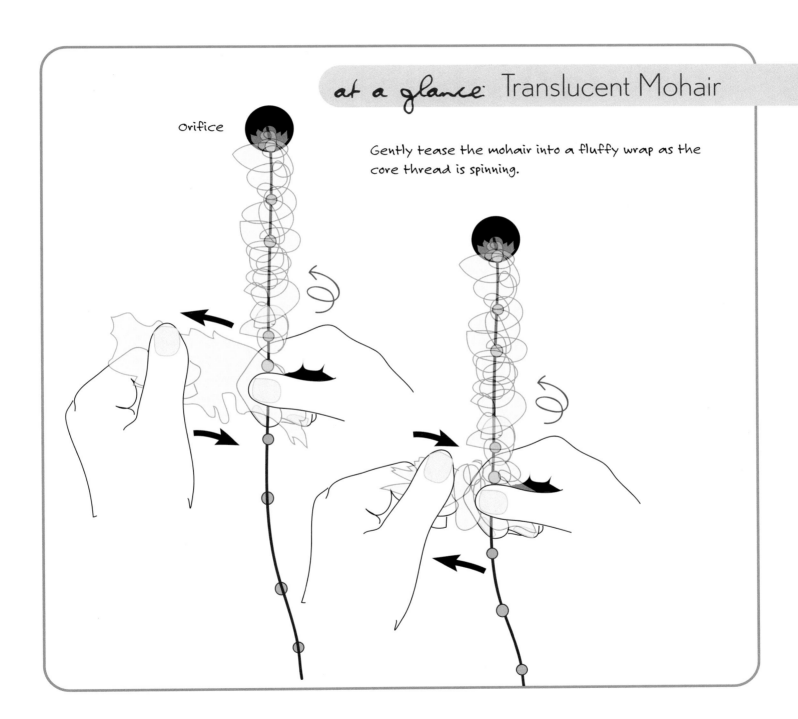

Orifice

Gently tease the mohair into a fluffy wrap as the core thread is spinning.

PUTTING IT ALL TOGETHER

This yarn was many years in the making; each technique within it was developed separately and through much trial and error. In Aura, five techniques are used to create a rich, complex, and beautiful yarn. This is a difficult yarn to make, and it is best to first master the five techniques separately before attempting to make this yarn.

Techniques used

Translucent Mohair (page 138)
Wrapped Yarn (page 78)
Semi-Felted Bubbles (page 114)

Aura Yarn

Materials

10 + oz (282.5 g) uncarded fiber, roving scraps, and semi-felted wool in miscellaneous colors

100 yd (91.5 m) core thread

2 oz (56.5 g) white mohair clouds

300 yd (274.5 m) novelty threads or lace-weight yarn

Spin!

Attach the core thread and some roving to the leader string and begin spinning a simple single for 3–4" (7.5–10 cm). This single should be just enough to make a section for tying off the skein later. Attach the novelty thread and spin 3–4" (7.5–10 cm) to secure it.

Grab a miscellaneous assortment of the uncarded fibers, roving bits, and semi-felted wool and place them in your lap. Now, take a quiet moment to ready yourself for the challenge. Breathe deep. Open your eyes … and begin.

Randomly grabbing chunks from the fiber in your lap, begin spinning them onto the core thread. Do not draft these fibers—simply spin them onto the core thread in their current state.

Allow the novelty thread to wind on between your hand and the orifice (see Wrapped Yarn, page 78). Now for the tricky part…As you are spinning the uncarded fibers, grab small, thinly drafted clouds of mohair and allow it to loosely wrap onto the forming yarn (see Translucent Mohair, page 138).

Everything should be happening simultaneously: spin the uncarded fiber onto the core while fluffing the mohair around the forming yarn; in the meantime the novelty thread is wrapping itself around the whole kit and caboodle near the orifice. Pay attention to the novelty thread to make sure it does not get stuck for too long in one spot. If it does get stuck, simply pull the thread forward with your hand until it begins to wind on evenly again. (It will by no means

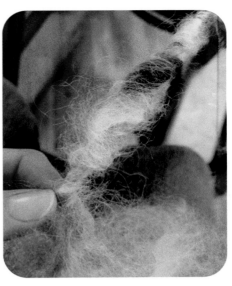

Three things happening at once: spinning the uncarded fiber, surrounding it with mohair, and novelty thread wrapping around the yarn close to the orifice

wrap perfectly even, and the irregularity is nice, just don't allow it to get too concentrated in one spot.)

Continue the process until the bobbin is full. Wind the yarn off onto a niddy noddy, tie in 4 or 5 places to prevent tangles, remove from the noddy, and soak in *very hot water* for about 15-20 minutes. Set the yarn on a yarn stretcher.

Pluckyfluff Advice Center: I've learned the hard way so you don't have to!

Think of Wool as Glue

Wool is to a spinner as duct tape is to a handyman. It can be used almost anywhere to fix anything. Wool's most valuable quality is its tendency to grab: it grabs onto itself and it grabs onto everything else around it. Its fibers have an abundance of scales that cling to each other and create a bond. Wool also has a great memory, meaning it can easily be set with hot water and it will hold its shape.

You can repair a break in your yarn by putting the severed ends together sandwiched between thin layers of well-drafted wool. Continue spinning and use your fingers to mold the wool around the break (think of manipulating clay on a pottery wheel). The wool will meld right into the yarn.

You can also use small clouds of wool to attach nonbinding materials, such as fabric, rubber, paper, etc., to your yarn.

Um ... how the heck is that going to fit through the orifice?

You'd be amazed. If it's soft, it can probably get through. The most important tool to have on hand when adding big elements to your yarn is the threading hook. This is the little hook that you thought was only used for fishing your leader string through the orifice. Not anymore! This is the wonder tool. If you have a big knot, a felt object, or anything else that is *not rigid*, you can feed the hook through the orifice from the backside; when the hook comes out the front, hook it around the large element and drag it back through the orifice and out the other side. It is helpful to keep some tension on the yarn between you and the hook, as you may need to pull the element back and forth a few times to work it through.

What if it is rigid or just too darn big?

Not a problem. If you have a bead or other item that just won't fit through the orifice you can *bypass* the orifice. Simply cut the yarn between the item and the orifice, then retie it at the bobbin. First, make sure that the item has at least 6" (15 cm) of spun yarn both in front and behind it. Break your unspun roving off, leaving just the item and the few inches (centimeters) of yarn. It is best to spin a very thin section about 6" (15 cm) ahead of the item; cut the yarn here (a thin yarn will make a more discreet knot). Keep the ends of the yarn pinched to prevent unraveling. Pull the bobbin-side yarn back out of the orifice and tie the two ends back together, then hand wind the item onto the bobbin. Using your threading hook, fish the end of the yarn from the bobbin side back through to your side of the orifice. Reattach your roving and continue spinning.

How should I prepare my materials for spinning?

Lay it all out. Your spinning will go a lot smoother if you prepare all your fiber ahead of time and stage it on a work surface near your wheel. If you know that you want to make a blue yarn with pink nubs, then separate all the blue roving into spinnable strips and all your pink into nub-sized chunks. Adding scraps? Put a pile of scraps on the work space. Not only does this make spinning more efficient but it also allows you to see all the elements together ahead of time and decide if they really work together or not. Most important, the less time you spend fussing with materials, the more open you'll be to creative whim.

How do I process raw wool?

Lay the raw fleece out on the floor and "skirt" it. This means remove all of the beyond-dirty sections, or wool that is caked in dung or mud or is too matted, or otherwise unusable.

Next, prepare a hot bath in a utility sink or tub (don't use your kitchen sink!) and add ¼ cup (60 ml) of degreasing dish soap. Gently add the wool and delicately submerge it. *Do not agitate* or the wool will felt. Let it soak overnight.

Remove the wool from the water and place it in the washing machine on the spin cycle until the water is removed.

Prepare a new hot bath with 1 tablespoon (15 ml) of mild laundry soap. Add the fleece and gently submerge. Allow the fleece to soak for an hour or so. Remove the fleece, place it in the washing machine, and spin out excess water. Repeat this step until the water from the bath runs clear (this could take as many as 5 or 6 baths if the fleece is really dirty).

On the final bath, do not add any soap. Add ¼ to ½ cup (60 to 120 ml) distilled white vinegar to the last rinse water. This will remove all extra suds and leave the wool soft and lustrous. Spin the fleece in the washing machine and then lay it out on an airy surface to dry (a wire shelf or basket).

Above: *Coral 2007,* Wood-fired porcelain with hand-dyed and spun mohair and merino knitted and felted. Britta Cruz, www.dreamlandart.com

Right: Fiber landscape by Melissa Baker, www.moustacheridesyarn.com

chapter 5

Blurring the Line

BETWEEN ART AND CRAFT

As long as there has been art there has been a debate over what constitutes art. Some see art in terms of absolutes; it either *is* or it *isn't* art. Others view it more subjectively. Nothing stirs these waters like the craft genres. Crafts are not fine art, yet they often embody great creativity. Crafts have their roots in function, yet almost always, inevitably, reach for a higher level of appreciation. Craftsmen and women have often sought to integrate ideas such as beauty and meaning into their craft.

So when does craft become art? There are as many answers to that question as there are people to ask it. Maybe it is not so important to ask *when* it becomes art, but to ask *how* it becomes art. *When* asks for a division between art and not art; a time when it wasn't and a time when it was. But asking *how* it becomes art leads us to examine the process that the craft goes through. A process is a holistic journey. A process is not black and white; it is an evolution through the grayscale. The craft of handspun yarn spans from pure functional yarn making to art. However, it is not the extremes of this range that are most interesting, it's what happens in between.

The yarn in this transformation zone between function and art does not declare itself as much as it instigates people to ask, "What is it? Can you use it? Do you just look at it?" It reveals more about the beholder than about the yarn itself. Two people will look at the exact same yarn, and one will see a perfectly functional material for funky mittens, while the other may see it as finished art in and of itself. The yarn in this gray area is the most energetic and elusive. It waves and fluctuates, and blurs the line between art and craft.

Yarn That Just *Is*: Yarn That Is Art

Era, Icelandic wool, mohair, Tencel, cotton, and sparkle spun with mohair boucle thread, vintage needlework, and nylons by Pluckyfluff

Left: Over-under-spun yarn in wool, mohair, sparkle, Lincoln locks, string, and scraps by Linda Scharf

Below: *Aura,* Miscellaneous wool bits surrounded by white mohair and wrapped in French novelty threads

What pushes a yarn unmistakably beyond the gray area of creative craft? Every now and then a yarn clearly transcends its yarn-ness and transforms into something altogether new. It has reached beyond mere craft when most people agree that it *Is*, just as it is. It is seen as a complete entity that needs nothing more, and does not want to be transformed beyond itself. A yarn has reached its fullest potential if using it would lessen it.

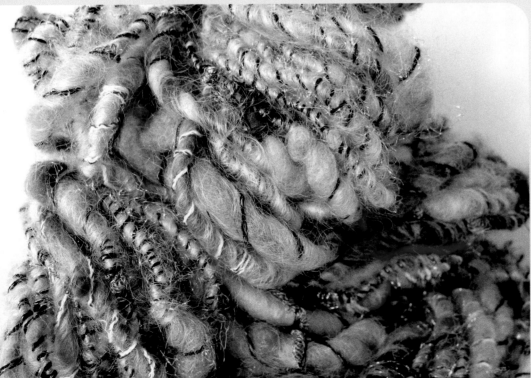

The Art of Handspun Yarn

Art That Is Yarn

There is no greater use for handspun yarn than as the material for art. In the hands of an artist, already creative yarn can take on meaningful, beautiful, and poignant forms.

Dreaded Corps Baleine, This is a life-size corset that fits the artist. The fabric is handwoven dreadlocks and handspun human hair yarn, stabilized with packing wire and backed with corduroy. It laces up with a Rapunzel-esque rope made of handspun hair yarn, all from one little girl who had her first haircut. It comments on the discomfort of naively trying to meet beauty standards, by Whitefeather.

CHRIS GILES

Top left: Single-ply wool yarn with yarn pompoms and vintage embroidered horse, by Pluckyfluff

Top Right: Fiber landscape by Melissa Baker, www.moustacheridesyarn.com

Left: Voodoo pincushion dolls, felted wool, handspun yarn, and uncarded locks, by Daniela Kloppmann, Felt Studio, www.feltstudio.co.uk, www.feltstudioUK.etsy.com

Freeform Crochet

There is no needlecraft genre better suited to creative handspun yarn than freeform crochet. At their core, creative spinning and freeform crochet share the same ideology: That rules are meant to be learned, then broken. That the form must be *brought out* of the material rather than imposed upon it. That every mistake is a discovery and should be integrated rather than erased. That the outcome is unknowable until you get there. That the final work is a visual record of the journey, with every decision, mistake, and idea visibly integrated into the whole.

Octi-Scarf by Linda Scharf

FREEFORM CROCHET AND HANDSPUN YARN

By Linda Scharf

A great starting place to get a feel for freeform crochet is the sadly out-of-print book, *The Crochet Workbook,* by James Walters and the late Sylvia Cosh, published in 1989. Many people took workshops and popularized techniques now referred to as freeform crochet, but James and Sylvia offered a philosophy (along with some techniques) of freeform crochet that is wide open and ever expanding.

Some people think of freeform as pattern-free crocheting, while others think it means joining small pieces of crochet doodles to form a bigger piece, such as wall hanging.

I think of freeform crochet as pure play using a crochet hook and just about any material: yarn, fabric, wire, plastic … the possibilities are endless, as shown by what so many artists have done. It is tuning in very deeply to the materials that one is working with to listen to what they want to be, what form wants to be created at that particular moment.

Freeform takes advantage of the natural uncensored way our brains can optimally work. It allows us to portray, in an uninhibited way, what is inside of us. It asks, "What if …?" What if I kept going with this line of crochet? What if I stopped now, continued, changed colors or yarns, made up stitches, turned the thing upside down, inside out, didn't think there was a right way, a wrong way, inserted the crochet hook anywhere and just started crocheting from there, or laughed at being "lost"?

Handspun yarn lends itself perfectly to freeform crochet. It's very likely that the handspun yarn has already been created with a free attitude, so every inch of the yarn is still alive with the artist's/spinner's response to the moment. The changes in color and texture call out to the freeform crocheter, asking to be appreciated and shown to their fullest expression. The freeformer can pull out loops to really show slubs and poofy areas, change direction to break up the tyranny of stripes, or make stitches more open to allow the textures of the handspun yarn to really shine.

The freeform crocheter works in collaboration with the spinner to create something unique to that partnership, something that would not have existed before this interaction. To be fully present in the moment, actively co-creating a small universe—isn't this a perfect way to experience the best of being human? Moving beyond the boundaries that we or society sometimes imposes on us, so that we can contribute to creating more joy in the world?

As James and Sylvia wrote in their book's introduction, "Free means being aware, being able to generate new options and to make fresh choices whenever we need." This philosophy is available to everyone—just get a crochet hook and begin anywhere!

Linda Scharf (www.stoneleafmoon.com) is an artist based in Boston, Massachusetts. An innovator in fiber arts and spinning, Linda is the founder of the first museum dedicated to the craft of creative spinning, www.theyarnmuseum.com.

Ana Voog

Ana Voog is a pioneer in art, crochet, and life. Currently the longest running live-cam girl to date, Ana's life is 24-hour art. Though she didn't invent freeform crochet, it is safe to say that she is the undisputed queen of it. She has pushed the genre to its fullest potential, creating unimaginable works and inspiring others to reach past all boundaries. Ana Voog is a major catalyst in the push to transform crochet from a craft to a major art form. Her works have been seen in MOMA NY, *Vogue K1*, *Dwell Magazine*, and on computer screens across the globe.

Ana Voog's journal

initial entry

i started crocheting May 21st, 2002.
my friend's husband's sister taught me the basic single stitch and from that moment onward, i became completely obsessed.
it even seems that somehow i am just accessing past knowledge. it feels like i have always known crochet. i am simply re-remembering it. the next day i wrote this in my livejournal:

22 may 2002 02:41pm

crocheting IS a fantastic analogy for life, as i knew it would be :)

where every action you take in life is a knot you make. what kind of actions determining the shape of the whole. you could make the same action over and over and you would come up with a sturdy basic structure but by learning a variety of knots, each done with discipline and intent, you make any shape you want for whatever purpose. by taking actions in life, each action done at the same time each day for the same duration each day you will produce the sturdiest most symmetrical shape. do this with intent and change your

Left: Freeform crochet sweater using cassette-tape yarn. The adjustable hood/collar is attached to the hair by the clips in the yarn. By Ana Voog, www.anacam.com/hats

Above: Single-ply wool and cassette-tape yarn spun with metal roach clips by Pluckyfluff

Freeform crochet hat with robins' eggs and wire circles by Anna Voog

shape/pattern/life? am i paying attention to what shape i am making by the actions i am doing? and is this a shape i want to create?

also, don't get so wrapped up in the details of your actions/knots, that you forget to step back and evaluate the greater picture of what you are making. there is a time and place for everything. balance is the key.

i now understand more completely the art of "mindfulness"

wow, all this insight from making one crazy hat/doily ... ummm.THING!

by the time i figure out how to actually MAKE something *I* will be the dalai lama! :) "

actions/knots when you want to create a new shape. but each action/knot you make becomes the foundation for all future shapes and actions. so make certain that the knot you make is the knot you want to base future actions on. you cannot go back and undo one particular knot without taking apart everything you have done so far. if you make a mistake, with creativity, you can improvise it into the pattern/shape and learn something new. and the entire shape/ pattern really has no absolute beginning or end.

so every time you make an action in life, ask yourself ... is this a knot i want and trust to hook my future actions into? will this knot/action compromise the integrity of my

livejournal entry, years later

i am wondering if anyone else here feels a deeper connection to something spiritual while they are crocheting because i do.
firstly, it's meditation to me. i am a pretty high-strung nervous person a lot, and crochet has really helped me stay grounded and calm down. secondly, when i'm crocheting, it feels like i am connecting to something really ancient and therefore that is also very grounding and it feels good to me to be connected in that way.

Right: Freeform crocheted and felted jacket by Anna Voog

Far right: Freeform crochet hoodie from wire-core yarn by Anna Voog
Yarn by Kathy Foster

(i know in crochet history they say it has not been around for a long time ... maybe i am just connecting to needlework in general).

also, it seems that crochet is just such a good analogy for so many things in life. the way things are interconnected. the way it is important to lay a good foundation. the way that there is joy in repetition. and the way that even a thousand-mile journey begins with one step. it's also good for cultivating focus, discipline, and patience.
and with free form it's good for trusting in yourself and the universe, following your heart, listening to your intuition, and not trying to force anything but let it be what it wants to be. to let go of attachment.
and like life, crochet seems to be more about the process than the final end result.

i also think there is a huge connection to even physics and higher mathematics. like string theory and sacred geometry.

i think that the process of crocheting a doily or a potholder could help to enhance spiritual enlightenment in the same way that tibetans create mandalas ... and so many other worldwide religions and belief systems.

journal entry 2-17-04

how to make a hat (or a spaceship)

when you start out learning to crochet something ...

start out using only crappy yarn u don't care about so you won't care if you make any mistakes. choose a plain kind of yarn (like good old white acrylic yarn that is nonfuzzy) so you can see your stitches.

then detach from all your expectations and goals of how you want your finished piece to look and sometimes even what you want it to be.

let it be what it wants to be and let it lead you on a journey, not the other way around :) that is most important.

leave in the "mistakes." almost everything i have ever made has led me to a better place than i thought i wanted to be when i left in the mistakes :)

almost like if you were building a house very slowly, so slowly that trees started sprouting up inside the structure of your house (trees=mistakes/serendipity). but you decide to not pull up the tree and you change your plans a bit and build around it and incorporate it in. pretty soon you have a lot of trees and the floor plans you had have to be rearranged as you go, so much so that the entire house is now a different shape than you had originally planned. but once you look back on what you have made you will see that your house is even more spectacular now than you ever could have imagined and you cannot imagine wanting a house without all of those trees growing through it. and the trees actually took you on a journey you did not expect

and you learned more about architecture than you would have learned if you had stuck to your original plans. and maybe your house isn't even a house anymore but a treefort or a spaceship :)

this is how i make my hats :)

Freeform crocheted and felted scarf by Anna Voog

Kathy Foster

Kathy Foster is a single-handed fiber artist from Vancouver, BC. She's been crocheting since 2000, when she took it up as a good sit-still hobby while recovering from a car crash that took her left arm and leg. Constantly inspired by just about everything, she dyes and spins her own yarn and brings it to life, usually in hat form. She uses her own self-taught technique she calls Adaptive Crochet. If she's not crocheting, she's washing dirty wool in the bathtub. When not washing wool, she's working away on a new felt thing or collecting bits and pieces to add into yarn.

Freeform crocheted hats by Kathy Foster, www.electrickat.com

Electric Kat

by Kathy Foster

While recovering from a car crash that took my left arm and leg, I was surfing around the Internet and came across Ana Voog's crochet. I had never seen anything like her hats before, and all I could think about was learning to crochet.

My boyfriend's mother taught me the single chain. At first I found it difficult, holding the crochet hook in the grip of my prosthetic hook-hand. I figured out how to work the yarn around the hook with my fingers. It's not the traditional form of crochet—I call it adaptive crochet. I hold the hook completely still. Sometimes I hold the hook between my knees or wedged against my body when I'm unable to wear my prosthetic.

Almost everything I make is done in a single chain stitch. One stitch leads to another; close your eyes and drift off while the yarn decides what it wants to be. That's what I love so much about freeform crochet. There are no rules to follow. As I sit and stitch I watch my work come to life right before my eyes. Each piece takes on a personality of its own. I let the yarn dictate every stitch. I never know what the next stitch will lead to. The possibilities are endless. The yarn is the star of the show. The first handspun yarn I'd ever worked with was from Pluckyfluff, and after using it all, I wanted to use was handspun yarn. My heart skipped and jumped around at the very thought of handspun yarns and I felt the need to make my work become completely my work. I needed to make my own yarns.

I didn't think I could do it, as handspinning is a very hands-on activity. I bought a used wheel, took a few classes to get the theory down, and spent many frustrating nights in front of my wheel, swearing at it, but eventually I figured out how to draft with my electric robot hand!! Now years later I can spin completely one-handed. I will throw just about anything into my drum carder and try to make it into yarn. I'm a woman *obsessed*!

Elaine Evans

Fiber artist Elaine Evans has been forging new ground with her innovative creations. Each item she creates is completely unique. Sculptural forms arise from the texture and colors of the wool and other fibers she brings together for her designs. Many items feature yarn that has been created by Elaine herself. She teaches freeform, beginning, and advanced crochet classes as well as spinning for people of all ages. She is a teacher for the Textile Mobile, an educational outreach program of the Textile Center of Minnesota.

FUZZYBUMBLEBEE: Fun fuzziness for the future.
Photo by Rich Ryan

chapter 6
Beautiful Asymmetry
PATTERNS AND PROJECTS

The question most often asked about non-traditional handspun yarn is, "Can you knit and crochet with it?" The answer is yes, you can. The more appropriate question, though, may be, "Can you follow a pattern with it?" Here is where it gets cloudy. The reason why most people can follow a pattern and get a predictable result is because they are using commercial yarn. Patterns depend on predictability. A commercial yarn, even if it's an "irregular" novelty yarn, is *never* random and will always repeat in a predictable way. Commercial yarns are made by machines, and machines follow repeating programs.

Nontraditional handspun yarn is inherently unpredictable because it is created by humans, so, by nature, the resulting yarn is more random. Handspun yarns are very likely to interrupt a pattern with an element that does not fit in and needs to be handled in a different way. This can very quickly lead to problems if you are focused on reproducing something exactly from a pattern.

The trick is to use the right yarn to suit your purpose. If you want an exact reproduction from a pattern, then use very regular commercial yarn or a traditionally spun handspun yarn. It's clean and neat, with no surprises, and you're guaranteed to get what you are looking for. However, trying to fit nontraditional handspun yarn into a rigid pattern will lead to frustration. This is not the fault of the pattern. A pattern is only made rigid by our own expectations. You *expect* your project to look like the picture. Expectation often leads to disappointment. So, when it comes to using handspun yarn, the key to happy knitting or crocheting is to embrace the unexpected.

The most rigid and symmetrical of patterns will divulge the very core nature of handspun yarn. Nontraditional handspun yarn will turn a rectangle into a wave every time. This is the spirit within the handspun yarn revealing itself. The grid can be its guideline but not its confine. Embrace this spirit and do the same in terms of your craft. Let your individual nuances, quirks, flaws, perspectives, and strengths—your *inherent unpredictability*—push your work beyond the grid and into a more organic, creative place.

Change the way you think about the relationship between yarn and pattern. Consider the pattern as more of a rough guideline rather than a set of unbreakable rules. Think of the yarn as a creative contributor to the project, not just a mere material. Traditionally, it is the knitting or crocheting that dominates the yarn. When using handspun yarn, allow the yarn to influence the knitting or crocheting at

times. Let the creation of the project be an interplay between the idea behind the pattern and the unique qualities of the yarn. Walk on the path of the pattern, but by all means follow the yarn off the trail if there is something more interesting to see.

This section includes a collection of patterns. Try them, tweak them, and then try some of your own devising.

Slouch Hat

This is a great slouchy hat that can be worn several ways: tall, slouchy, folded up, or pulled over your eyes for a little undisturbed snooze time. The most important design element is to make it unusually tall; aside from that, this hat can be interpreted in many ways. Try ribs, cables, or stockinette. Make it kind of tall and be a little slouchy, or make it really tall for super slouchiness!

Knitting Skills Required

Cast on (CO)
Knit (k)
Purl (p)
Bind off (BO)
Knit 2 together (k2tog) decrease
Purl 2 together (p2tog) decrease

Size

RIBBED HAT
Circumference: 21¾" *(55 cm)*
Length: 11" *(28 cm), uncuffed;* 9" *(23 cm) cuffed*

STOCKINETTE STITCH HAT
Circumference: 20" *(51 cm)*
Length: 10" *(25.5 cm) unrolled;* 9" *(23 cm) with lower edge rolled*

Materials

Ribbed hat: *About 120 yd (114 m) chunky thick and thin singles (50% silk, 50% camel carded with small amounts of black silk noil and rainbow wool)*

Stockinette stitch hat: *About 110 yds (100 m) thick and thin thread-plied yarn (100% natural brown CMV)*
Ribbed hat: *Size 11 (8 mm) set of 4 or 5 double-pointed needles*
St st hat: *Size 10 (6 mm) set of 4 or 5 double-pointed needles*
Change needle size as necessary to accommodate your yarn and gauge
Tapestry needle
10 markers for St st hat

Gauge

Ribbed hat: 11 sts = 4" (10 cm) in k5, p5 rib using size 11 (8 mm) needles
St st hat: 12 sts = 4" (10 cm) in circular St st (knit every row), using size 10 (6 mm) needles

The Fiber

Used here: Silk/camel blend; 100% natural brown wool

The Yarn

Thick 'n' thin soft-spun single in 50/50 silk and camel down, carded with little bits of rainbow wool and black silk noil

Ribbed hat

With larger needle cast on 60 sts, join sts in circle taking care not to twist sts. Work in k5, p5 rib for 38 rnds, or until work measures about 9" (23 cm).

Crown shaping
Rnd 1: K2tog in the center of each k5 section, work p5 sections as usual—54 sts.
Rnds 2 and 4: Work even in patt without decreasing.
Rnd 3: P2tog in the center of each p5 section, work k5 sections as usual—48 sts.
Rnd 5: K2tog using the first 2 sts in each knit section, work even in purl sections—42 sts.
Rnd 6: P2tog using the first 2 sts in each purl section, work even in knit sections—36 sts.
Rnd 7: Repeat row 43—30 sts.
Rnd 8: Repeat row 44—24 sts.
Rnd 9: K2tog in each knit section—18 sts.
Rnd 10: P2tog in each purl section—12 sts.

Girl's Hat: Thick 'n' thin soft-spun single in ribbed-slouch pattern.
Boy's Hat: Thick 'n' thin thread-plied natural brown wool in stockinette stitch.

Rnd 11: K2tog around—6 sts rem. Cut yarn, leaving 4" (10 cm) tail. Thread tapestry needle with yarn tail and insert through 6 rem sts. Gently pull yarn tail to draw sts together and close top of hat. Weave in yarn tails to WS and secure.

Stockinette Stitch Hat

With smaller needle cast on 60 sts, join sts into circle taking care not to twist sts. Knit all rnds until hat measures about 8" (20.5 cm) with lower edge unrolled.

Crown shaping
Rnd 1: *Knit 4, k2tog, place marker; rep from * 10 times—50 sts
Rnds 2, 4, 6, and 8: Knit to end of rnd.
Rnd 3: K3, k2tog; rep from * 10 times—40 sts.
Rnd 5: K2, k2tog; rep from * 10 times—30 sts.
Rnd 7: K1, k2tog; rep from * 10 times—20 sts.
Rnd 9: K2tog to end of rnd—10 sts.
Rnd 10: K2tog to end of rnd—5 sts.
Cut yarn, leaving 4" (10 cm) tail. Finish off same as ribbed hat.

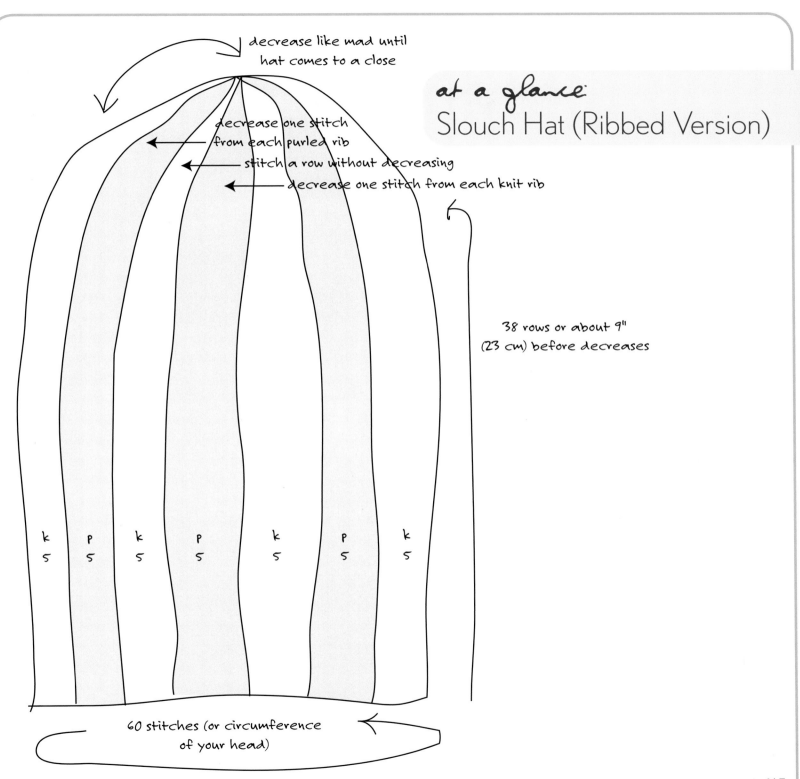

decrease like mad until
hat comes to a close

decrease one stitch
from each purled rib

stitch a row without decreasing

decrease one stitch from each knit rib

38 rows or about 9"
(23 cm) before decreases

k 5   p 5   k 5   p 5   k 5   p 5   k 5

60 stitches (or circumference
of your head)

Unraveled Scarf

This stunning and unusual scarf looks complicated but it is a surprisingly quick and easy project.

Knitting Skills Required

Cast on (CO)
Knit (k)
Purl (p)
Make 1 (m1) increase

Size

Circumference: *About 18" (45.5 cm)*
NOTE: *This pattern stitch will easily expand several inches (centimeters) to pass over the head.*
Length: *3½" (9 cm), knitted section only, from CO to beginning of pulled loops*

Materials

100 – 125 yds (91.5 – 114 m) 2-ply traditional handspun, about 8 wpi
Shown here: Blend of 60% natural gray Corridale wool, 40% Possum
Size 9 (5.5 mm) set of 5 double-pointed needles. Change needle size as necessary to accommodate your yarn and gauge
Tapestry needle or crochet hook, any size
Stitch marker

Gauge

About 15 sts = 4" (10 cm) using size 9 (5.5 cm) needles

PHOTOS BY KYLE PARKER

Beautiful Asymmetry **167**

Scarf

Cast on 70 sts. Place marker and join into round, taking care not to twist stitches.

Rnd 1: *K5, p5; rep from * to end of rnd.

Rnds 2 – 18: Rep rnd 1.

Rnd 19 (increases): *K1, m1, k4, p5, k5, p5; rep from * 2 times more, then work last 10 sts as k1, m1, k4, p5—74 sts.

Rnd 20 (increases): *K6, p1, m1, p4, k5, p5; rep from * 2 times more, then work last 11 sts as k6, p1, m1, p4—78 sts.

Rnd 21: Knit first st, pulling the yarn through until a loop of yarn hangs 12–18" (30.5 to 45.5 cm) long. Let the extended loop fall off needle. Rep this process, creating loops through all stitches, varying the loop length for each stitch. Pull the last loop through at end of rnd. Cut the yarn, leaving a 48" (122 cm) tail. Fold the tail in half to create a loop then tie the final 6" (15 cm) of this strand to the last stitch, securing the tail with a discreet overhand knot. Weave the yarn end into the scarf with a crochet hook or tapestry needle.

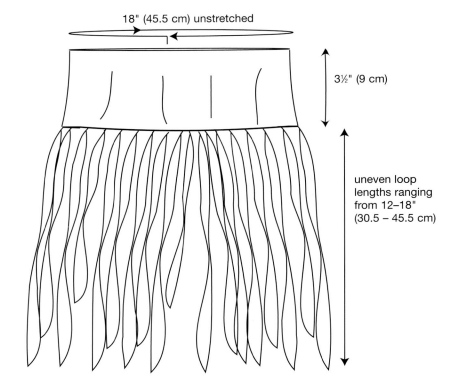

18" (45.5 cm) unstretched

3½" (9 cm)

uneven loop lengths ranging from 12–18" (30.5 – 45.5 cm)

at a glance: Unraveled Scarf

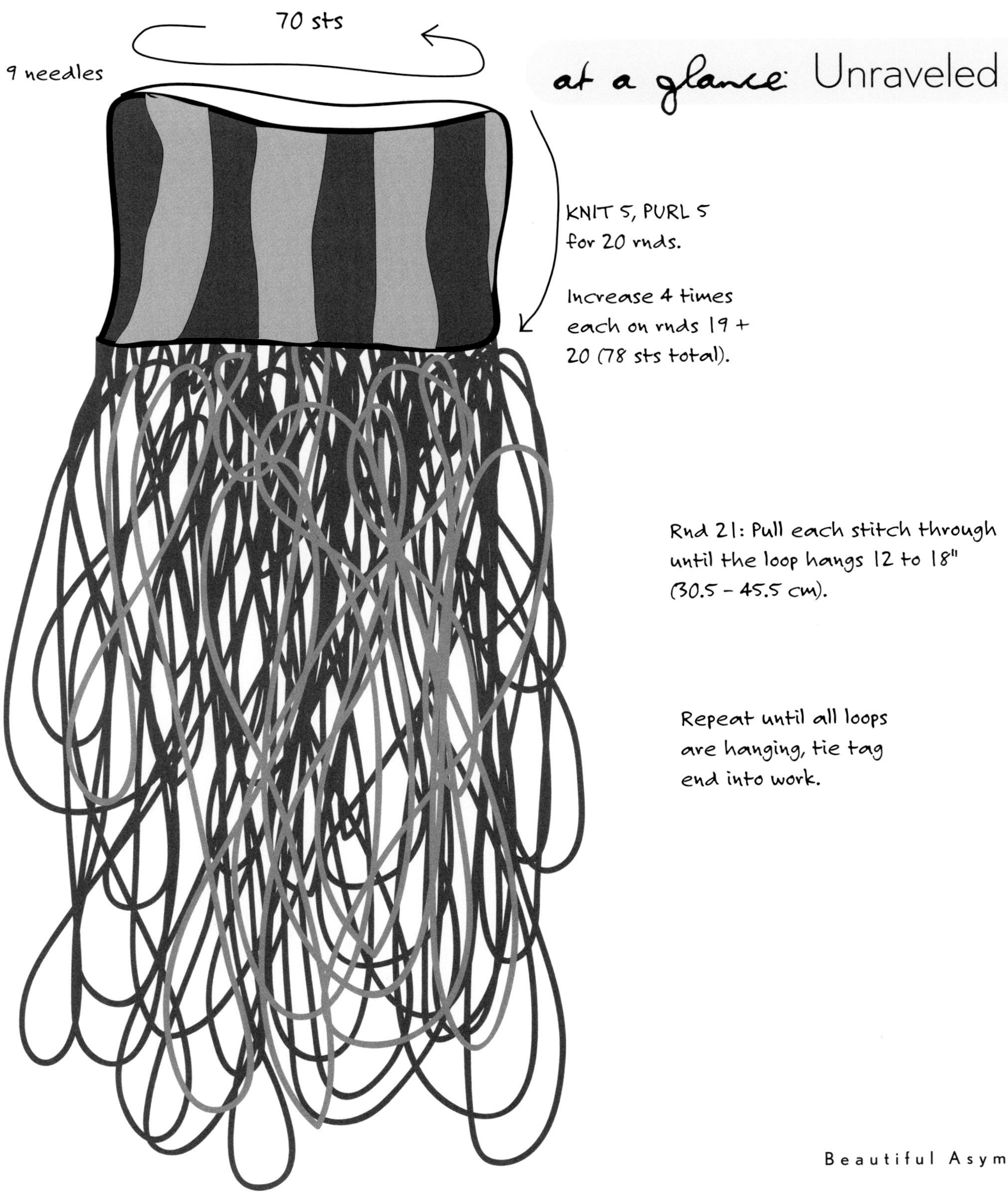
70 sts
US size 9 needles
KNIT 5, PURL 5
for 20 rnds.
Increase 4 times
each on rnds 19 +
20 (78 sts total).
Rnd 21: Pull each stitch through
until the loop hangs 12 to 18"
(30.5 – 45.5 cm).
Repeat until all loops
are hanging, tie tag
end into work.

Pretty 'n' Punk Neck Cuff

Pearls and ribbon give this edgy design a sweet appeal.

Knitting Skills Required

Cast on (CO)

Garter st

Knit (K)

Bind off (BO)

Size

Length: *4" (10 cm)*

Width: *16" (40.5 cm) overlapped with buttons closed*

Materials

40 – 50 yds (36.5 – 45.75 m) handspun yarn

Size 10 (6 mm) needles. Change needle size as necessary to accommodate your yarn and gauge

2 buttons, about 3/4" (2 cm) circumference

About 24" (61 cm) silk ribbon to tie on as bow

Tapestry needle

Gauge

14 sts = 4" (10 cm) using size 10 (6 mm) needles in garter st

Neck cuff design, yarn, and knitting by Stephanie Nericcio, Stitch Ewe Yarns, www.TimewornTrades.com; bustier by Armour sans Anguish, www.armoursansanguish.com

The Yarn

Simple single-ply natural gray wool with recycled pink silk strips, pink sparkle, pink satin ribbon, and strings of faux pearls

Neck Cuff

Cast on 14 sts. Work in garter st (knit every row), until cuff is long enough to wrap around the wearer's neck, plus about 1" (2.5 cm) overlap for buttons. BO all sts. Weave in loose ends to WS of work to secure.

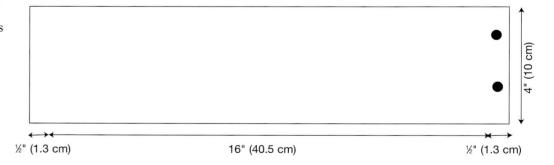

½" (1.3 cm)   16" (40.5 cm)   ½" (1.3 cm)   4" (10 cm)

Stephanie attached the 2 buttons about ½" (1.3 cm) in from the left short edge. She did not make buttonholes, but simply pushes the buttons through the openings between stitches. When the cuff is closed, thread silk ribbon through top front edges and tie into a bow.

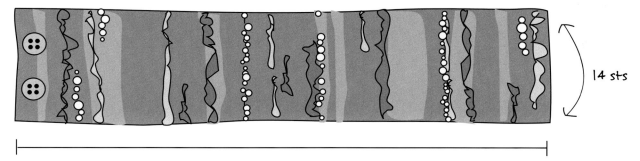

14 sts

Long enough to wrap around neck + 1" (2.5 cm) for buttons

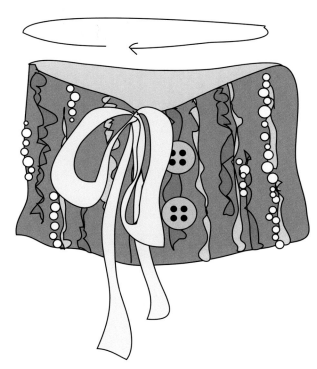

KYLE PARKER

Taffy Scarf

Spin a jumbo-size thick and thin yarn candy-striped with a ribbon yarn with silver neps to make this easy cable project.

Knitting Skills Required

Cast on (CO)

Knit (k)

Purl (p)

Cable 6 front (c6f): slip 3 sts from left needle onto cable needle and hold in front of work. K3 sts from left needle, k3 sts from cable needle.

Bind off (BO)

Size

Length: *60" (152.5 cm)*
Width: *4½" (11 cm)*

Materials

Handspun jumbo yarn (see spinning instructions page 76), (100% merino wool plied with ribbon yarn); about 200 yds (182 m)

Size 17 (12.75 mm) needles. Change needle size as necessary to accommodate your yarn and gauge

Tapestry needle

Gauge

7½ sts = 4" (10 cm) in St st using size 17 (12.75 cm) needles

The Yarn

Jumbo thick and thin handspun plied with commercial ribbon yarn, by Drucilla

Scarf

Cast on 8 sts.

Rows 1 and 3 (RS): K1 (edge st), k6, k1 (edge st).

Rows 2 and 4 (WS): K1, p6, k1.

Row 5: K1, slip next 3 sts to cable needle, hold in front, k3 from left needle, knit 3 from cable needle, k1.

Row 6: Rep row 2.

Rep these 6 rows for pattern. Work even in cable patt until scarf measures about 60" (152.5 cm). BO all sts.

tip: Do not hold rigidly to cabling every 6th row (row 5 of pattern) if your yarn dictates otherwise. If the yarn goes into an extended thin section, you may want to cable sooner, as thin sections will elongate with the weight of the scarf. I cabled on row 3 once or twice when the yarn was thinner than usual. Doing so allowed me to maintain the shape and texture better.

KYLE PARKER

at a glance Taffy Scarf

Cable 6 center stitches every row 5 of pattern

front (RS):

(k)(k)(k)(k)(k)(k)(k)(k)

back (WS):

(k)(p)(p)(p)(p)(p)(p)(k)

Repeat pattern until scarf is about 60" (152.5 cm) long.

Twizzler Scarf, Go Diagonal!

This simple project creates a dramatic look with bold diagonal lines and highly textured thread-plied yarn.

Knitting Skills Required

Cast on (CO)

Garter st (knit every row)

Bind off (BO)

Bar increase, also called K1f&b (1 st increase): knit into the front loop of st, then, without removing st from needle, knit into the back loop

Double bar increase, also called K1f,b&f (2 st increase): knit into the front loop of st, then knit into the back loop, then back into the front loop before removing st from needle

Size

Length: 64" (162.5 cm)
Width: 6" (15 cm)

Materials

70 yd (64 m) thread plied yarn with coils, yarn A (see page 96)

50 yd (46 m) mohair clouds yarn, yarn B (see page 138)

optional: 120 yds (110 m) self-striping yarn instead of using two different yarns

Size 11 (8 mm) needles. Change needle size as necessary to accommodate your yarn and gauge

Tapestry needle

Gauge

About 8 sts = 4" (10 cm) using size 11 (8 mm) needle in garter st

The Yarn

Pattern by Sophia, Yarn Over Manhattan, Violiknit at www.yarnovermanhattan.blogspot.com; Twizzler thread-plied yarn by Pluckyfluff; knitted by Cindy Cafaro

Thread-plied crazy-carded wool with coils

Scarf

NOTE: If working with 2 yarns, work 18 rows (9 ridges) with yarn A, join yarn B and work 4 rows (ridges) with yarn B. Continue yarn changes, working 6 rows (3 ridges) yarn A, followed by 4 rows (2 ridges) yarn B.

CO 1 st.
Row 1: K1f,b&f—3 sts
Row 2 and all WS rows: Knit.
Row 3: K1f&b, k1, k1f&b—5 sts.
Row 5: K1f&b, knit to last st, k1f&b—7 sts.
Continue in this manner, increasing in first and last sts on RS rows and knitting the WS rows until scarf is the width you want (Cindy increased until she had 19 sts). Beginning with yarn B, change yarns as noted above, or follow your own formula if using 2 different yarns.
Next RS row: K1f&b, knit across row to last 2 sts, k2tog.
Next row (WS): Knit.
Rep last 2 rows for about 50" (127 cm) or desired length. Change to yarn A only. If you don't have enough yarn A to complete scarf end, continue using yarn B in stripe pattern for a few more stripes before completing scarf end with yarn A only.

Next RS row: K2tog, knit across row to last 2 sts, k2tog.
Next row (WS): Knit.
Rep these last 2 rows until 3 sts remain.
Next RS row: K3tog. Cut yarn leaving 4" (10 cm) tail and fasten off last st. Cut second yarn leaving 4" (10 cm) tail. Thread tapestry needle and weave in ends to WS, or weave in along outside edges to secure.

Braid Hat

Try a new twist on classic dangles with this Rapunzel-inspired hat.

Knitting Skills Required

Cast on (CO)
Stockinette stitch (St st): knit all rounds
Bind off (BO)

Size

Height: *9" (23 cm)*
Circumference: *23" (55.5 cm)*

Materials

100 yd (91.5 m) thread-plied merino yarn
with coils
10–20 yds (9–18 m) lace-weight commercial
mohair
4 strips of vintage fabric, each about 48"
(122 cm) long and ½" (1.3 cm) wide
Size 13 (9 mm) set of 5 double-pointed
needles. Change needle size as necessary
to accommodate your yarn and gauge
Tapestry needle

Gauge

8 sts = 4" (10 cm) using size 13
(9 mm) needles in St st (knit every
row).

The Yarn

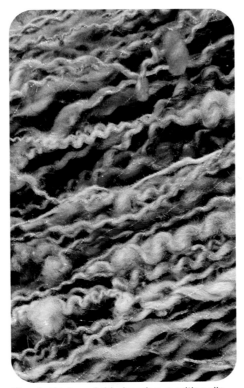

Simple thick and thin handspun with coils
and thread plied. About 8 wpi.

Hat

With dpns cast on 46 sts. Join sts in
round, being careful not to twist sts.
Knit each rnd until work measures
about 6" (15 cm) from CO, dec 1 st
on last rnd—45 sts.

Crown shaping
Rnd 1: *K7, k2tog; rep from * 4 times
more—40 sts.
Rnds 2, 4, 6, 8: Knit.
Rnd 3: *K6, k2tog; rep from * 4 times
more—35 sts
Rnd 5: *K5, k2tog; rep from * 4 times
more—30 sts.
Rnd 7: *K4, k2tog; rep from * 4 times
more—25 sts.
Rnd 9: *K3, k2tog; rep from * 4 times
more—20 sts.
Rnd 10: *K2, k2tog; rep from * 4
times more—15 sts.
Rnd 11: *K1, k2tog; rep from * 4
times more—10 sts.

Rnd 12: K2tog around—5 sts. Cut yarn, leaving 6" (15 cm) tail. Thread tapestry needle and insert through center of rem 5 sts. Pull gently to close top of hat. Weave in loose ends to WS.

Braids

Set your swift to 44" (112 cm). Using the remaining thread-plied yarn and a selection of lace-weight commercial mohair, wind these yarns onto the swift in the following ratio:

Thread-plied yarn: 20 wraps
Commercial lace-weight mohair: 4 wraps
Remove the yarns from the swift, lay the yarns flat on a hard surface, and make a single cut through the loops. This will provide you with a bundle of yarns about 44" (112 cm) in length. Split the bundle evenly into two groups. Add 2 fabric strips to each bundle (fabric strips will be slightly longer than yarns).

NOTE: Mixing the mohair and fabric strips into the braids is a subtle way to distinguish the braids from the hat fabric. Without the change in texture, the project becomes monotone.

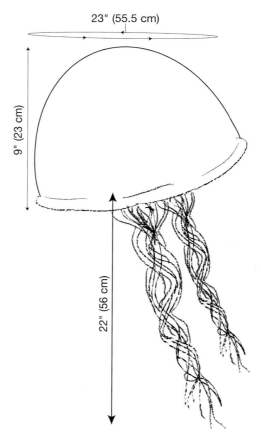

23" (55.5 cm)

9" (23 cm)

22" (56 cm)

*Using a crochet hook and working with 3 or 4 strands at a time, pull the strands through a stitch loop about 3 rows up from the CO edge, working from the *inside (WS)* of the hat to the outside. (It's better not to strand through the bottom row or CO edge because it pulls the edge of the hat down in an unattractive way.)

Pull the strands through to halfway so there are equal lengths on each side. Still working from the *inside* of the hat, hook the strands through the neighboring loop, grab them, and pull them back to the WS. The strands should be securely threaded through the work and hanging in equal lengths. Adjust strands if necessary to make them equal lengths*. Repeat from * to * with another batch of 3 or 4 strands, passing through the next stitch loop. Continue in this manner until a span of about 4" (10 cm) is covered. Separate yarns and fabrics into 3 sections and braid. Tie braid at bottom with a stripe of fabric to secure.

Put the hat on and adjust so that the braid hangs directly over one ear. Locate the stitch loop in the hat that is centered directly over the *other* ear; this is where you will begin threading the next batch of yarns. Repeat from *, threading strands 2" (5 cm) in each direction from this starting point. Braid and tie off.

at a glance: Braid Hat

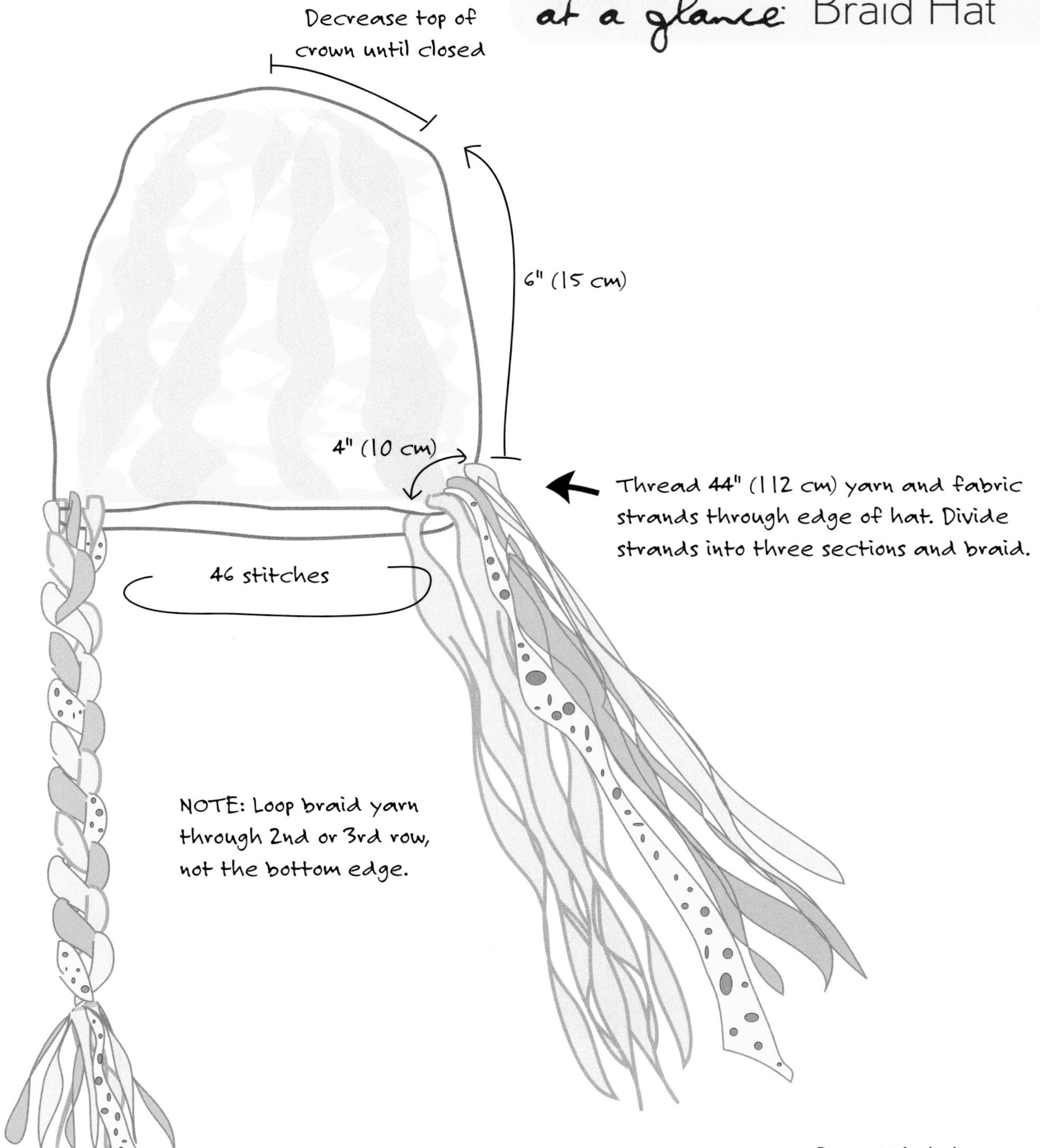
Decrease top of crown until closed
6" (15 cm)
4" (10 cm)
Thread 44" (112 cm) yarn and fabric strands through edge of hat. Divide strands into three sections and braid.
46 stitches
NOTE: Loop braid yarn through 2nd or 3rd row, not the bottom edge.

Recycled Cleansuit Scarf

This scarf is manly through and through! Cleansuits are available in many colors, from blue/gray to orange. No need to buy a new one; used ones are easy to come by and have been softened by years of hard work. Look for a suit with interesting elements that can be shown off in the yarn, such as a name badge, tags, printed words or numbers, patches, or repairs.

Knitting Skills Required

Cast on (CO)
Knit (k)
Purl (p)
Stockinette stitch (St st): Knit 1 row, purl 1
    row
Reverse St st: Purl 1 row, knit 1 row

Size

Length: *66" (167.5 cm)*
Width: *4" (10 cm)*

Materials

1 used mechanic's cleansuit (overalls)
Sturdy core thread
Size 17 (12.75 mm) needles. Change needle
    size as necessary to accommodate your
    yarn and gauge
Crochet hook, any size, or tapestry needle

Gauge

8 sts = 4" (10 cm) in St st using size
17 (12.75 mm) needles

The Yarn

80 – 100 yds (73 – 91.5 m) cleansuit yarn. Begin with a used mechanic's cleansuit. Using heavy-duty scissors, separate the seams, zippers, and pockets from the flat panels of the material. OPTIONAL: Save the seams and zippers, as they could make good fringe material.

Tear all of the remaining material into ½" (1.3 cm) strips. The easiest way to do this is to make little "starting" cuts with the scissors about ½" (1.3 cm) apart, along the edge of the material. Then simply tear each strip from the main piece. Once the entire suit is salvaged, use a sturdy thread, yarn, or string that matches the color of the strips, and core-spin a fabric yarn (see page 128 for spinning fabric instructions).

Scarf

Cast on 8 sts. *Work in St st for 2 to 5 rows, then work 1 row in reverse St st. Rep from * until scarf measures about 66" (167.5 cm) from CO edge, or until you run out of yarn. BO all sts. With tapestry needle or crochet hook, weave loose ends to WS and secure.

Purl

KNIT

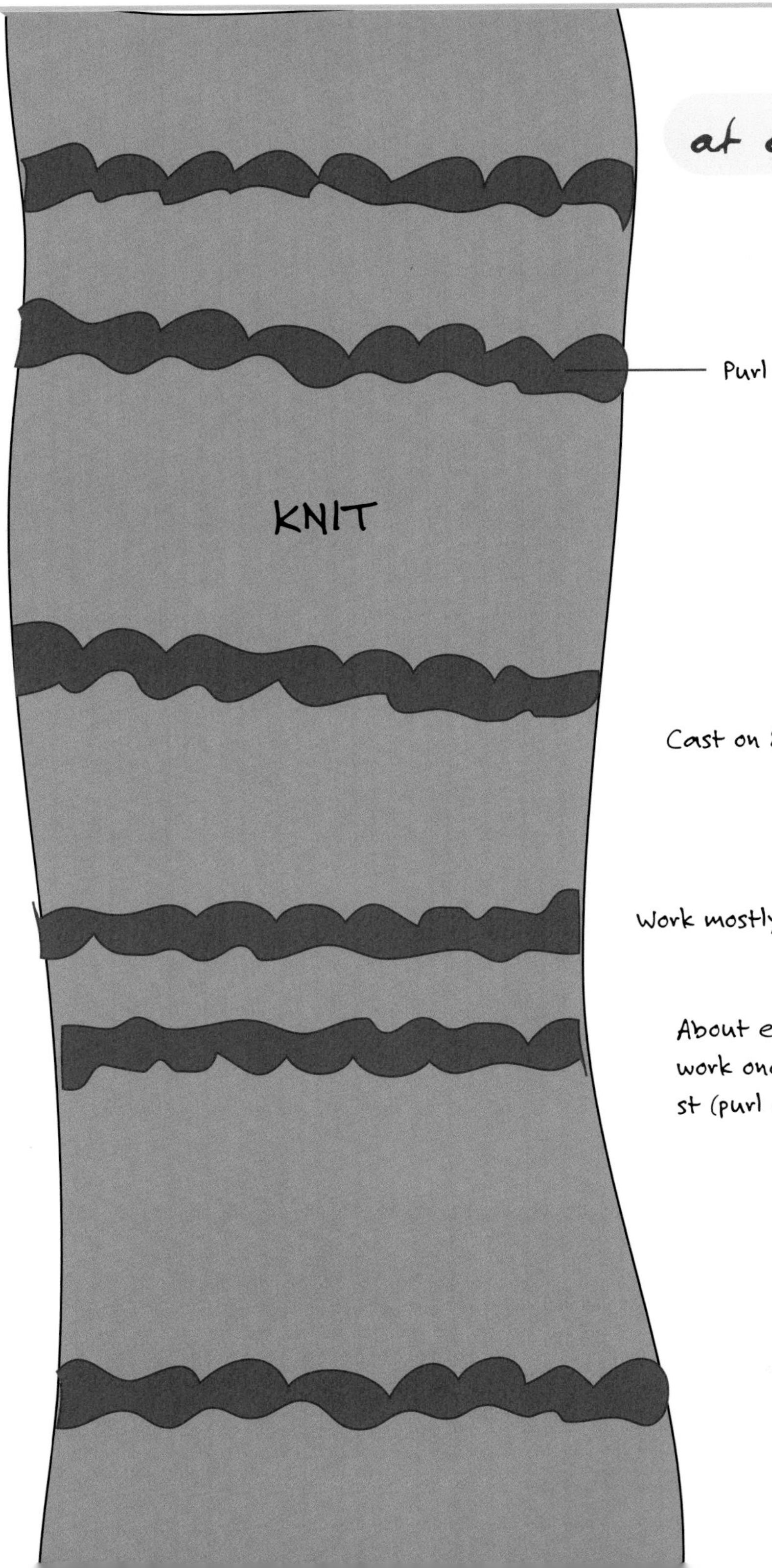

Cast on 8 stitches

Work mostly in Stockinette stitch.

About every 2–5 rows
work one row reverse St
st (purl on RS).

Cleansuit Hoodie

Recycled utilitarian material is juxtaposed with the finest of unprocessed wool locks for a dramatic effect.

Knitting Skills Required

Cast on (CO)
Knit (k)
Purl (p)
Knit 2 together (k2tog) decrease
Backward loop CO (increase)

Crochet Skills Required

Chain (ch)
Slip st (sl st)
Double crochet (dc)

Size

Opening around face: *21" (53.5 cm)*
Width (not incl mohair locks):
    8" (20.5 cm)
Total Length (including crochet and
    fabric strap): *13" (33 cm)*

Materials

*100 yd (91.5 m) recycled mechanic's
    cleansuit yarn (see Recycled Cleansuit
    Scarf instructions, page 187).*
*About 1 yd (1 m) Extreme tailspun mohair
    yarn (see Extreme Tailspin, page 134)*
*About 2 yds (2 m) scrap white commercial
    yarn to attach tailspun yarn to hoodie*
Size 17 (12.75 mm) knitting needles
Size P/15 (10 mm) crochet hook
Size Q (15 mm) crochet hook
*Change needle size as necessary to
    accommodate your yarn and gauge*
Tapestry needle

Gauge

8 sts = 4" (10 cm) in St st using size
17 (12.75 mm) needles

The Yarn

Yarn spun from a shredded mechanic's
cleansuit

Hoodie Sides (make 2)

With recycled cleansuit yarn, CO 14 sts. Beg with WS row, work in St st for 13 rows.

Row 14 (RS): K1, k2tog, k5, k2tog, k4—12 sts.

Row 15: P1, p2tog, purl to end—11 sts.

Row 16: K1, k2tog, knit to end—10 sts.

Row 17: BO all sts.

Make second side same.

Center Panel

With recycled cleansuit yarn, CO 14 sts. Beg with WS row, work in St st for 16 rows.

Row 17 (WS): P5, p2tog, p6—13 sts.

Row 18 (RS): Knit.

Row 19: P5, p2tog, p5—12 sts.

Row 20: K1, k2tog, knit to end—11 sts.

Row 21: P1, p2tog, purl to end—10 sts.

Row 22: Knit.

Row 23: Purl.

Row 24: K5, inc 1 using backward loop method, k4—11 sts.

Row 25: Purl.

Row 26: K1, inc 1 using backward loop method, knit to last st, inc 1 using

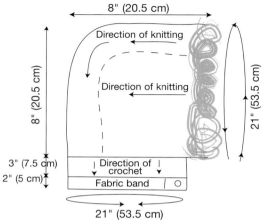

8" (20.5 cm)

Direction of knitting

Direction of knitting

8" (20.5 cm)

21" (53.5 cm)

3" (7.5 cm)

2" (5 cm)

Direction of crochet

Fabric band

21" (53.5 cm)

backward loop method, k1—13 sts. Work even in St st until piece measures about 16" (40.5 cm) from CO, or until center panel is long enough to attach around 2 sides of side panel.

Attach Panels

Using smaller crochet hook and cleansuit yarn, align both side pieces with the center panel (RS facing) and working on WS of work, seam pieces together with slip st.

Neck

Using larger size crochet hook and cleansuit yarn, working around lower edge of hoodie, work as follows:

Row 1: Begin 4 sts from front edge, slip st into sts around lower edge of hood until 4 sts from other front edge. Turn work.

Row 2: Ch 3, 1 dc in each sl st. Turn work.

Row 3: Sl st in each st. Fasten off.

Collar

Using scraps from the cleansuit (pictured: snaps/button holes from front closure and part of the collar), cut and sew a band (about cuff-width) long enough to wrap around base of hood plus cover front of neck. Utilize pre-existing buttons and holes to make the closure in front of neck. Using sewing machine with a denim needle, attach collar along the base of the hood. You will need a sewing machine that allows you to sew without any pressure on the foot. Otherwise, handstitch the collar on using buttonhole thread.

Attach Mohair Yarn

With smaller crochet hook, commercial waste yarn, and WS facing, ch st around the face edge of the hood and attach the mohair yarn about every 3 or 4 sts. Gently pull all mohair locks to RS around the front edge as necessary.

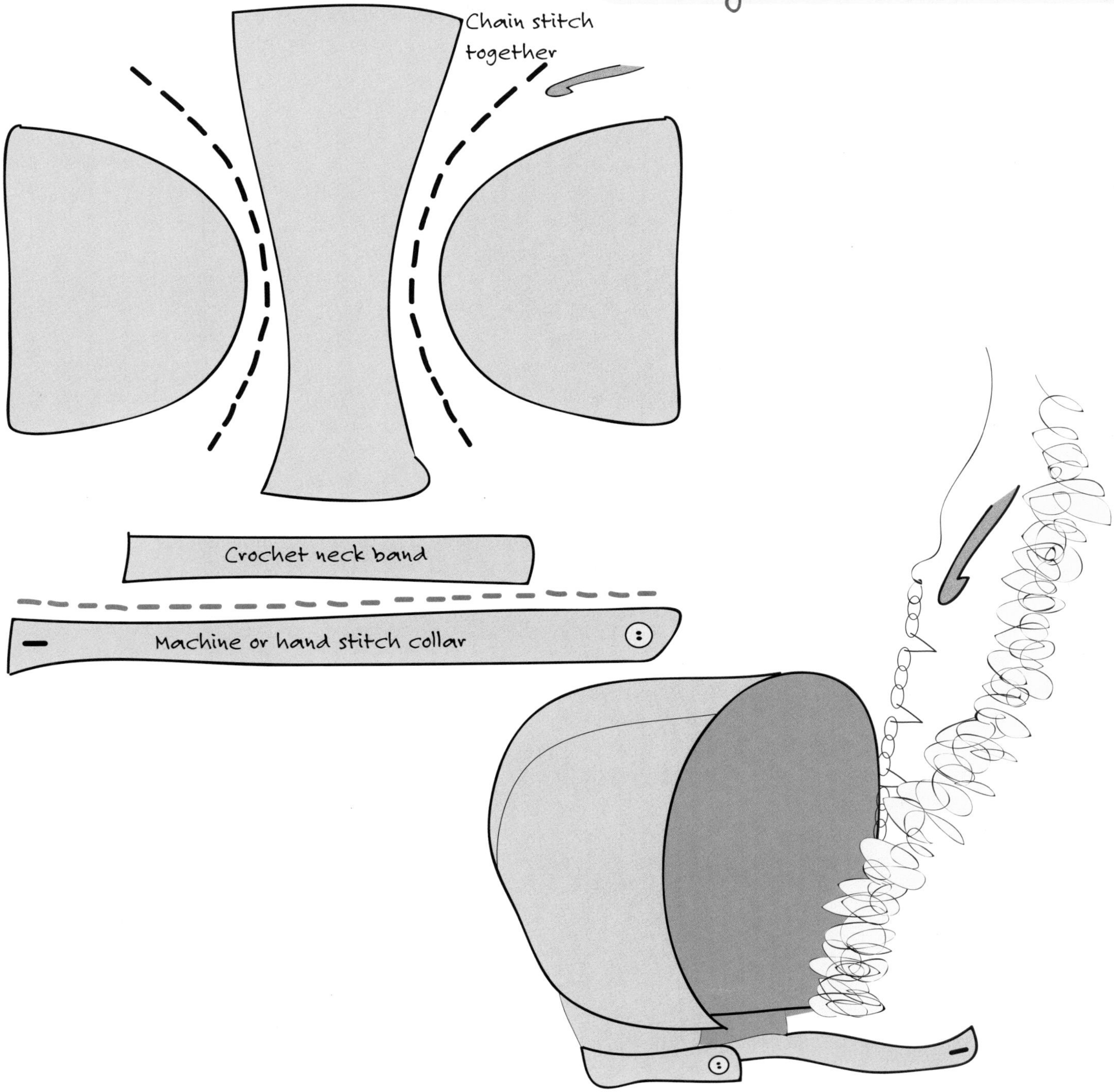

Chain stitch together

Crochet neck band

Machine or hand stitch collar

Snuggle Shrug

Extra soft and bulky Jumbo yarn makes this shrug perfect warmer for winter.

Knitting Skills Required

Cast on (CO)
Knit (k)
Purl (p)
K2, p2 ribbing
Bind off (BO)

Size

Length: *9" (23 cm)*
Circumference at neck edge:
   28" (71 cm)
Circumference at lower edge:
   32" (81.5 cm)

Materials

120 yd (110 m) soft-spun thick 'n' thin
   wool yarn
5 yd (4.5 m) silk ribbon, about
   ½" (1.3 cm) wide
Size 11 (8 mm) circular needle,
   24" (60 cm) long
Size 15 (10 mm) circular needle, same
   length as smaller needle for lower sec-
   tion. Change needle sizes as necessary
   to accommodate your yarn and gauge
Tapestry needle

Shrug design by Deborah Dant ; thick 'n' thin
handspun wool/angora yarn by Drucilla

Gauge

5 sts = 4" (10 cm) using size 15
(10 mm) needles in k2, p2 rib

The Yarn

Very thick 'n' thin handspun merino wool,
striped with fine gold metallic thread, small
nubs of Angora are randomly spun throughout, by Drucilla.

Shrug

With thick 'n' thin yarn and size 11 (8
mm) needle, cast on 40 sts. Join into
circle, taking care not to twist sts.
Work in rnds of k2, p2 rib. When
there are extra thin lengths in the
yarn, join the ribbon to work together
with the yarn, leaving 6" (15 cm) tails
when you join the ribbon. It's not necessary to complete the entire rnd with
ribbon; when yarn thickness increases
cut the ribbon leaving 6" (15 cm) tail,
and work in established patt with yarn
only. Change to larger needles when
shrug measures about 7" (18 cm) from
CO edge, and continue in established
rib patt until shrug measures 9"
(23 cm) from CO. BO all sts in ribbon
only. Secure all ribbon tails by tying
them around sts on RS of work, and
making half-loop bows. Weave in yarn
tails to WS and secure.

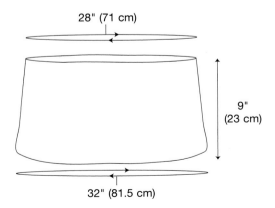

28" (71 cm)

9"
(23 cm)

32" (81.5 cm)

Elephant Poncho

The elephant is crocheted as an appliqué that is simply whipstitched to the finished poncho. Sparkle pom-pom yarn makes it a garment you won't have to wrestle your child to wear!

Crochet Skills Required

Chain (ch)
Slip st (sl st)
Single crochet (sc)
Half double crochet (hdc)

Size

Length: 11½" (29 cm)
Neck edge circumference: 20" (51 cm)
Lower edge circumference:
    42" (106.5 cm)

Materials

About 7 yd (6.5 m) soft yarn with body
    (yarn C)
70 yd (64 m) handspun thick 'n' thin single
    with pom-poms (yarn B)
1 ball Crystal Palace Merino Frappe (80%
    superfine merino, 20% nylon; 140 yd
    [128 m] per 50 g ball), color #012b New
    Latte (yarn A)
Size H/7 (4.5 mm) crochet hook. Change
    hook size as necessary to accommodate
    your yarn and gauge
Tapestry needle
Sewing needle and matching sewing thread

Gauge

14 hdc = 4" (10 cm) using size H/7 (4.5 cm) crochet hook with yarn A.

The Yarn

Thick 'n' thin wool handspun single with sparkly pom-poms

Poncho design by Tsia Carson, www.supernaturale.com; pom-pom yarn handspun by Jenny Neutron Star, www.jennyneutronstar.com

Poncho

NOTE: Poncho is worked from neck down to lower edge. Shaping is made on each rnd by working 3 sts in 1 at the center front st, and 3 sts in 1 at the center back st, increasing each rnd by 4 sts.

With yarn C, ch 70, join chain into circle with slip st. Make sure the chain isn't twisted.

Cut yarn C and join yarn B (leave 3" [7.5 cm] yarn tails when changing yarns to weave in later).

Rnd 1: Ch 2 (does not count as hdc), work 1 hdc in each of next 17 chs, work 3 hdc in next ch, work 1 hdc in each of next 34 chs, work 3 hdc in next ch, place marker, work 1 hdc in each of next 17 chs. Join rnd with sl st to top of ch-2—74 sts.

Rnd 2: Ch 2, hdc in next 18 hdc, 3 hdc in next st, hdc in next 36 hdc, 3 hdc in next st, hdc in next 18 hdc. Join rnd with sl st to top of ch-2—78 sts.

Rnd 3: Ch 2, hdc in next 19 hdc, 3 hdc in next st, hdc in next 38 hdc, 3 hdc in next st, hdc in next 19 hdc. Join rnd with sl st to top of ch-2—82 sts. Cut yarn B and join yarn A.

Rnd 4: Ch 2, hdc in next 20 hdc, 3 hdc in next st, hdc in next 40 hdc, 3 hdc in next st, hdc in next 20 hdc—86 sts.

Rnd 5: Ch 2, hdc in next 21 hdc, 3 hdc in next st, hdc in next 42 hdc, 3 hdc in next st, hdc in next 21 hdc—90 sts.

Rnd 6: Ch 2, hdc in next 22 hdc, 3 hdc in next st, hdc in next 44 hdc, 3 hdc in next st, hdc in next 22 hdc—94 sts.

Rnd 7: Ch 2, hdc in next 23 hdc, 3 hdc in next st, hdc in next 46 hdc, 3 hdc in next st, hdc in next 23 hdc—98 sts. Cut yarn A and join yarn B.

Cont in this manner, working 2 increases each in the center st of both front and back as in previous rnds. Change yarns as follows:

Rnd 8: Yarn B.

Rnds 9–17: Yarn A.

Rnds 18–20: Yarn B—150 sts.

Rnd 21: Join yarn C, ch 1, sc in each st around (no increases made on this rnd). Join rnd with sl st. With threaded tapestry needle, weave in ends to WS.

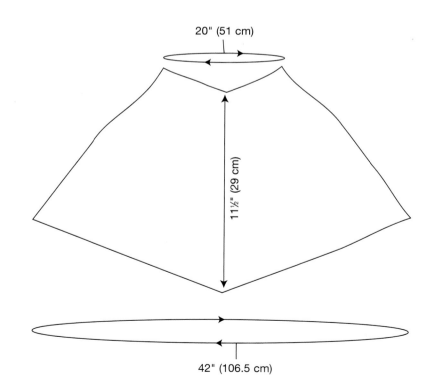

20" (51 cm)

11½" (29 cm)

42" (106.5 cm)

Tsia Carson

Elephant appliqué

With yarn B and using the stencil provided, work in sc and sl st to freeform the elephant. Work from left to right, first making the head and then the body. When finished, pin elephant to front of poncho; when elephant is positioned to your liking, thread sewing needle with sewing thread and whipstitch elephant in place. Remove all pins.

OPTIONAL: If you have any yarn B left over, appliqué a freeform butterfly, and attach the same way as elephant.

Spincycle Third Wave Harf

This pattern is the perfect design to show of the subtle elegance of traditional handspun yarn.

Knitting Skills Required

Cast on (CO)

Backward loop (e) cast on

Knit (k)

Purl (p)

Bind off (BO)

Stockinette stitch (St st): Knit 1 row, purl 1 row

Garter st: Knit all rows

Provisional CO

Kitchener St

Cable 8 front (c8f): Slip 4 sts from left needle onto cable needle and hold in front of work. K4 sts from left needle, k4 sts from cable needle

Size

One size fits all

Materials

3 skeins Spincycle Yarns light worsted-weight yarn, 120 yds (110 m) per skein

Size 9 (5.5 mm) needles. Change needle size as necessary to accommodate your yarn and gauge

Few yards of smooth waste cotton yarn for provisional cast on

2 stitch markers

1 stitch holders

Tapestry needle

Gauge

18 sts = 4" (10 cm) in St st on size 9 (5.5 mm) needles

The Yarn

Spin a simple worsted-weight yarn, about 12–13 wpi, either singles or 2-ply.

Hints

If you aren't comfortable with the provisional cast on and/or Kitchener st, the project works out fine if you make a regular CO, and finish the back seam with fake grafting. The only drawback is a visible seam.

Design and yarn by Kate Bürge and Rachel Price, Spincycle Yarns, www.spincycleyarns.com

Hood

Using a length of smooth waste cotton yarn and the provisional CO method of your choice (I prefer the crochet CO methods), CO 122 sts. The edging is worked in a simple cable pattern between garter st borders, as follows:

Row 1: K22, place marker (pm), k78, pm, k22.

Rows 2, 4, 6: K7, p8, k7, slip marker (sl m), p78, sl m, k7, p8, k7.

Rows 3 and 7: K22, sl m, k78, sl m, k22.

Row 5: K7, c8f, k7, sl m, k78, sl m, k7, c8f, k7.

Row 8: Rep row 2.

Rep above 8 rows until hood measures 9" (23 cm) from CO, ending with a RS row completed. If you want a deeper hood, continue in patt for another inch (2.5 cm), or to desired depth.

Separate for Scarf Ends

Once the hood is the desired depth and beg on WS row, work the first and last 22 sts in patt while working the middle 78 sts in garter st (knit all 78 sts on both RS and WS rows). Work 3 rows more, using garter st for the middle 78 sts (this will prevent

the brim from rolling). On the 5th row (WS), work first 22 sts in patt and place these sts on holder, BO the middle 78 sts, remove markers, work the rem 22 sts (this number incl st on right needle after the last BO) in patt.

First scarf end

Work even on these 22 sts, which are now one end of the scarf, in the established cable patt until it measures 25" (63.5 cm).

Make button holes

Beg after completing a row 8 of cable rep, work 2 rows in garter st across all 22 sts. On the 3rd garter row, k4, BO 5th and 6th sts, work to last 8 sts, BO 17th and 18th sts, knit rem 4 sts (this incl st on right needle after the last BO). On the 4th row, knit across, using the backward loop CO to replace sts that were bound off on the preceding row. Knit one more row in garter st, and then BO all sts.

Second scarf end

Pick up sts from holder and rejoin yarn. Work second scarf end same as first for 25" (63.5 cm). After completing row 8 of cable, work 5 rows in garter st. BO all sts.

Finishing

Carefully remove the waste cotton yarn from provisional cast on, picking up the sts as you go along. Once all sts are on one needle, slip half of them onto the second needle. Fold your harf in half down the middle of the hood (see Assembly Instructions, page 203) and, using a tapestry needle threaded with about 36" (91.5 cm) of yarn, Kitchener st the seam together. Weave in all tails to WS.

Try on your harf, wrapping each scarf end around your neck and matching up the ends so that the corners meet and overlap. Mark the scarf end where the buttons should go and sew them on opposite the button holes. Block if necessary.

Assembly instructions

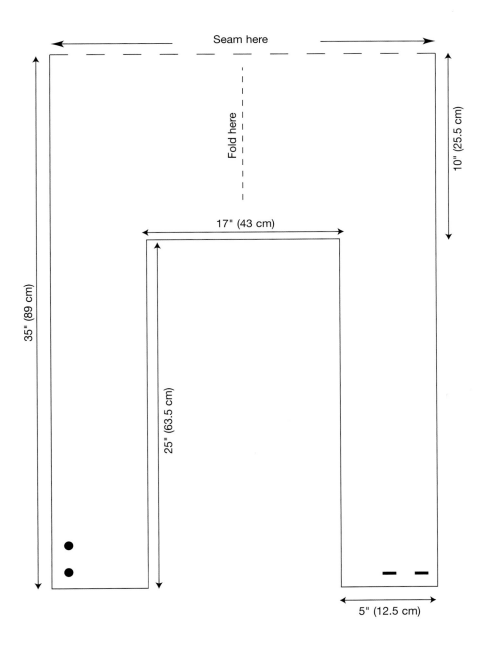

Seam here

Fold here

35" (89 cm)

17" (43 cm)

25" (63.5 cm)

10" (25.5 cm)

5" (12.5 cm)

Spincycle Poncho

This sweet and simple design shows off the natural beauty of handspun yarn without overwhelming it. This poncho was created by Spincycle Yarns and features their worsted-weight yarn in natural hues.

Knitting Skills Required

Cast on (CO)
Knit (k)
Purl (p)
Bind off (BO)
Stockinette stitch (St st): Knit 1 row,
    purl 1 row

Size

26" (66 cm) wide, 15" (38 cm) long

Materials

5 skeins Spincycle Yarns worsted-weight
    yarn, single or 2-ply 120 yds (110 m) per
    skein; 5 skeins
Size 9 (5.5 mm) needles
Change needle size as necessary to accom-
    modate your yarn and gauge
Tapestry needle

Gauge

18 sts = 4" (10 cm) in St st on size 9
(5.5 mm) needles

The Yarn

Spin a simple worsted-weight yarn, about 12 wpi, either singles or 2-ply.

Poncho

Cast on 117 sts. Work in St st until panel measures about 15" (38 cm) from CO edge. BO all sts loosely. Make second panel same.

Assembly Instructions

Lay the two panels flat as shown below. Using a tapestry needle threaded with a length of yarn, stitch together "A" from the first panel and "A" from the second panel. Then stitch together "B" from the first panel and "B" from the second panel. Weave in loose yarn tails to WS of work. Block poncho, if necessary.

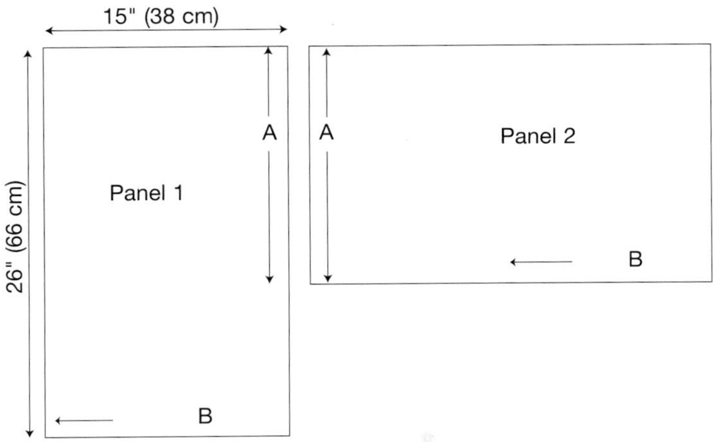

Design and yarns by Kate Bürge and Rachel Price, Spincycle Yarns, www.spincycleyarns.com

15" (38 cm)

26" (66 cm)

Panel 1

A

A

Panel 2

B

B

Shredded Scarf

The perfect use for secondhand scarves or handkerchiefs, shredded silk adds texture to this intricate scarf.

Knitting Skills Required

Cast on (CO)
Knit (k)
Purl (p)
Garter st: Knit all rows
Stockinette stitch (St st): Knit 1 row, purl 1 row
Reverse St st: Purl 1 row, knit 1 row
Wrapping yarn around needle multiple times
Bind off (BO)

Size

Length: 45" (114.5 cm), not including fringe
Width: 5" (12.5 cm)

Materials

100 yd (91.44 m) shredded scarf yarn (see Start to Finish, page 26)
15-20 strips torn silk fabric (we used an old silk scarf), each strip about 12" (30.5 cm) long by ½" (1.3 cm) wide
Sizes 13 (9 mm), 11 (8 mm), and 10½ (6.5 mm) knitting needles
Tapestry needle

Gauge

Not really important.

Section One

The first design concept within this scarf is a repetition of three shapes: waves, hourglasses, and ovals. Each is made with the same set of stitches, only in a different order. Once you become comfortable making the shapes, you can work them into your scarf in any order you like. They will naturally balance out if paired properly. Think of each wave, hourglass, or oval as a puzzle piece, and you need to make a rectangle or square. A left wave over a right wave will make a square. An oval next to an hourglass will also make a square. Keep this in mind as you knit to ensure that in the end, the scarf will hang straight and be balanced.

With size 13 (9 mm) needles, cast on 12 sts. Work 2 rows in Garter st.

Make left wave
Row 1: (K1 wrapping yarn around needle 3 extra times) 3 times, (k1 wrapping yarn around needle 2 extra times) 3 times, (k1 wrapping yarn around needle 1 extra time) 2 times, k4.
Row 2: Knit, dropping all extra yarn wraps from needle (this produces the elongated sts).
Rows 3 and 4: Knit.

Make right wave
Row 1: K4, (k1 wrapping yarn around needle 1 extra time) 2 times, (k1 wrapping yarn around needle 2 extra times) 3 times, (k1 wrapping yarn around needle 3 extra times) 3 times.
Row 2: Knit, dropping extra wraps from needle.
Rows 3 and 4: Knit.

Make hourglass
Row 1: (K1 wrapping yarn around needle 3 extra times) 2 times, (k1 wrapping yarn around needle 2 extra times) 2 times, (k1 wrapping yarn around needle 1 extra time) once, k2, (k1 wrapping yarn around needle 1 extra time) once, (k1 wrapping yarn around needle 2 extra times) 2 times, (k1 wrapping yarn around needle 3 extra times) 2 times.
Row 2: Knit, dropping extra wraps from needle.
Rows 3 and 4: Knit.

Make oval (inverse hourglass)
Row 1: K1, (k1 wrapping yarn around needle 1 extra time) once, (k1 wrapping yarn around needle 2 extra times) 2 times, (k1 wrapping yarn around needle 3 extra times) 4 times, (k1 wrapping yarn around needle 2 extra times) 2 times, (k1 wrapping yarn around needle 1 extra time) once, k1.
Row 2: Knit, dropping extra wraps from needle.
Rows 3 and 4: Knit.

Repeat these shapes and rows in any order until scarf measures 24" (61 cm) from CO.

tip: Any of these shapes can be tweaked to make large or small waves: simply wrap the yarn around the needle more or fewer times than noted in the previous instructions.

Section 2

The second design concept is that the scarf begins airy and organic on one end and evolves into a dense knit with a regimented pattern on the other. Change to size 11 (8 mm) needles and increase 1 st in the center of the row. Continue to make shapes as you did in section one; however, make the shapes smaller by working one wrap fewer in each segment, and working more regular knit sts as needed to complete the 13-st rows. Also, change the number of rows worked after row 2 to 4 rows in St st instead of Garter st. Continue section 2 until scarf measures 36" (91.5 cm) from CO edge.

Section 3

The third and last design concept completes the scarf, and is worked entirely in St st and reverse St st, without any shape rows.
Change to size 10½ (6.5 mm) needles and increase 1 st in the center of the row—14 sts.
Rows 1 and 3: Knit.
Rows 2 and 4: Purl.
Row 5: Purl.

Row 6: Knit.
Work rows 1–6 for a total of 18 rows.
Rows 19 and 21: Knit.
Row 20: Purl.
Row 22: Knit.
Row 23: Purl.
Work rows 19–23 for a total of 10 rows.
Rows 29 and 32: Purl.
Rows 30 and 31: Knit
Work rows 29–32 for a total of 20 rows or until scarf measures about 45" (114.5 cm) or desired length from CO edge.
Bind off all sts.

Fringe

Tie seven or eight 24" (61 cm) yarn lengths to CO edge of "organic" end of scarf, randomly spaced. Fill in remaining space with a few of the 12" (30.5 cm) strips of silk fabric tied to CO edge. Tie remaining silk strips to the BO edge of scarf, making bows at the edge of the work and leaving the ends trailing loose. If you have any remaining silk, tear strips and tie to scarf randomly several rows from the edge, leaving ends trailing over the fringe edge.

how to make a wave

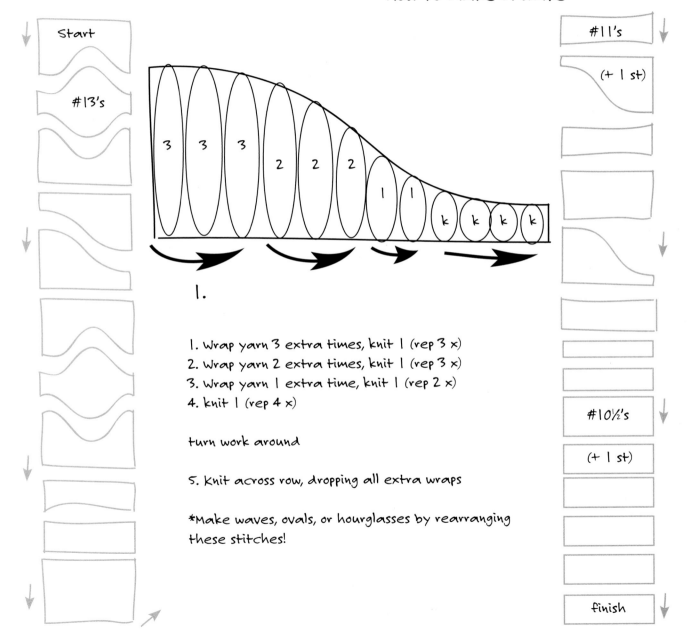

1.

1. Wrap yarn 3 extra times, knit 1 (rep 3 x)
2. Wrap yarn 2 extra times, knit 1 (rep 3 x)
3. Wrap yarn 1 extra time, knit 1 (rep 2 x)
4. knit 1 (rep 4 x)

turn work around

5. Knit across row, dropping all extra wraps

*Make waves, ovals, or hourglasses by rearranging these stitches!

Secret Stripe Gauntlets

This project demonstrates how you can work small amounts of handspun of varying wpi into a complete project by combining the handspun yarn with commercial yarns. In this example, the bold and regular striping of the commercial yarn is a perfect contrast to the soft, irregular, organic look of handspun.

Knitting Skills Required

Cast on (CO)
Stockinette stitch in rounds: Knit every rnd
Backward loop CO
Knit 2 together (k2tog)
Slip slip knit decrease (ssk)

Size

Total Length (with cuffs pulled open): 23"
 (58.5 cm)
Circumference of hand at knuckles:
 7½" (19 cm)

Materials

60 yd (55 m) bulky thread-plied yarn
About 110 yd (101 m) single-ply wool
 (about 14 wpi)
40 yd (36.5 m) red commercial yarn,
 light worsted-weight
40 yd (36.5 m) white commercial yarn,
 light worsted-weight
Size 11 (8 mm), size 10½ (6.5 mm), and size 9
 (5.5 mm) sets of 5 double-pointed needles
Change needle sizes as necessary to
 accommodate your yarn and gauge
Tapestry needle
Waste yarn

NOTE: The wpi of the single-ply yarn would normally indicate using a smaller size needle than the one specified here. However, this yarn is very bouncy and varies somewhat in thickness, so a larger than normal needle size was used to compensate. The mitt hand section could also be worked in a thicker yarn, something closer in wpi to the commercial yarns, or with two strands held together as one. If you opt for this, the number of increases made when the single-ply yarn begins can be reduced.

Gauge

16 sts = 4" (10 cm) in St st using size 9 (5.5 mm) needles and commercial yarn

Cuff yarn: Bulky 2-ply blend of wool, dog hair, aluminum, and felted bits by Kathy Foster, www.electrickat.com

Hand section of mitt: Single-ply natural brown wool yarn. "Natural" by Rachael-Marie, www.knittydirtygirl.com

Cuffs

Using bulky handspun and size 11 (8 mm) double-pointed needles, cast on 24 sts. Divide sts onto 4 needles, join work in circle taking care not to twist sts.

Rnds 1–21: K3, p3 rib to end of rnd.

Rnd 22: Change to size 10½ (6.5 mm) dpns, knit 1 rnd with bulky yarn.

Rnds 23–26: Change to size 9 (5.5 mm) dpns, join red commercial yarn, knit to end. Cut red yarn leaving 4" (10 cm) tail.

Rnds 27–30: Join white commercial yarn, knit to end. Cut white yarn leaving 4"(10 cm) tail.

Rep rnds 23–30 another 3 times (36 rnds), then work rnds 23–26 once more.

Mitts

Join single-ply handspun yarn, and continuing with size 9 (5.5 mm) dpns, work as follows:

Rnd 1: Knit to end of rnd.

Rnd 2: *Using backward loop method, co 1 st, k3; rep from * to end of rnd—32 sts.

Rnd 3: Knit to end of rnd.

Rnd 4: *K4, inc 1; rep from * to end of rnd—40 sts.

Rnds 5–11: Knit to end of rnd.

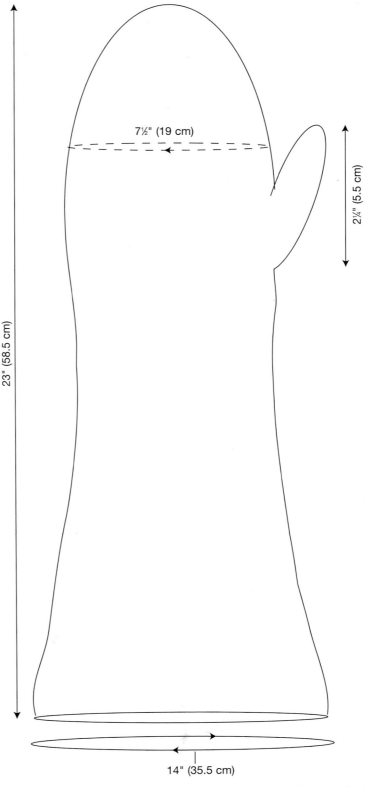

7½" (19 cm)

2¼" (5.5 cm)

23" (58.5 cm)

14" (35.5 cm)

Thumb and Mitt Top

NOTE: The thumb is positioned on the side edge, which means the mitts can be worn on either hand.

Rnd 12: K6 sts, slip these sts onto a strand of waste cotton yarn to hold (half of thumb sts). Using backward loop method, CO 6 sts on front of needle #1 to replace the thumb sts, knit the 6 CO sts, then knit to end of rnd—40 sts.

Work even on 40 sts until mitt just reaches the tip of your pinkie.

Hand Shaping

Rnd 13: (K1, ssk, k14, k2tog, k1) twice—36 sts.

Rnd 14: (K1, ssk, k12, k2tog, k1) twice—32 sts.

Rnd 15: (K1, ssk, k10, k2tog, k1) twice—28 sts.

Rnd 16: (K1, ssk, k8, k2tog, k1) twice—24 sts.

Rnd 17: (K1, ssk, k6, k2tog, k1) twice—20 sts.

Rnd 18: (K1, ssk, k4, k2tog, k1) twice—16 sts.

Rnd 19: (K1, ssk, k2, k2tog, k1) twice—12 sts.

Rnd 20: (K1, ssk, k2tog, k1) twice—8 sts.

Cut yarn, leaving 6" (15 cm) tail, thread tapestry needle and insert through rem 8 sts twice, pulling tail gently to close top of mitt. Weave tail to WS and secure.

Complete Thumb

Remove 6 thumb sts from waste yarn and slip onto a dpn. Join yarn, with second dpn pick up and knit 8 sts from CO above thumb sts—14 sts. Divide sts onto 3 needles.

Next 2 rnds: Knit.

Next rnd (dec 2 extra sts): K6, ssk, k4, k2tog—12 sts.

Work even in rnds on 12 sts until thumb measures about 2" (5 cm) or desired length to mid-nail.

Next rnd: *K1, k2tog; rep from * to end of rnd—8 sts.

Next rnd: *K2tog; rep from * to end of rnd—4 sts.

Cut yarn, leaving 6" (15 cm) tail. Thread tail on tapestry needle and insert through rem sts twice. Pull gently on tail to close top of thumb. Weave tail to WS and secure. Make second mitten the same.

at a glance: Secret Stripe Gauntlets

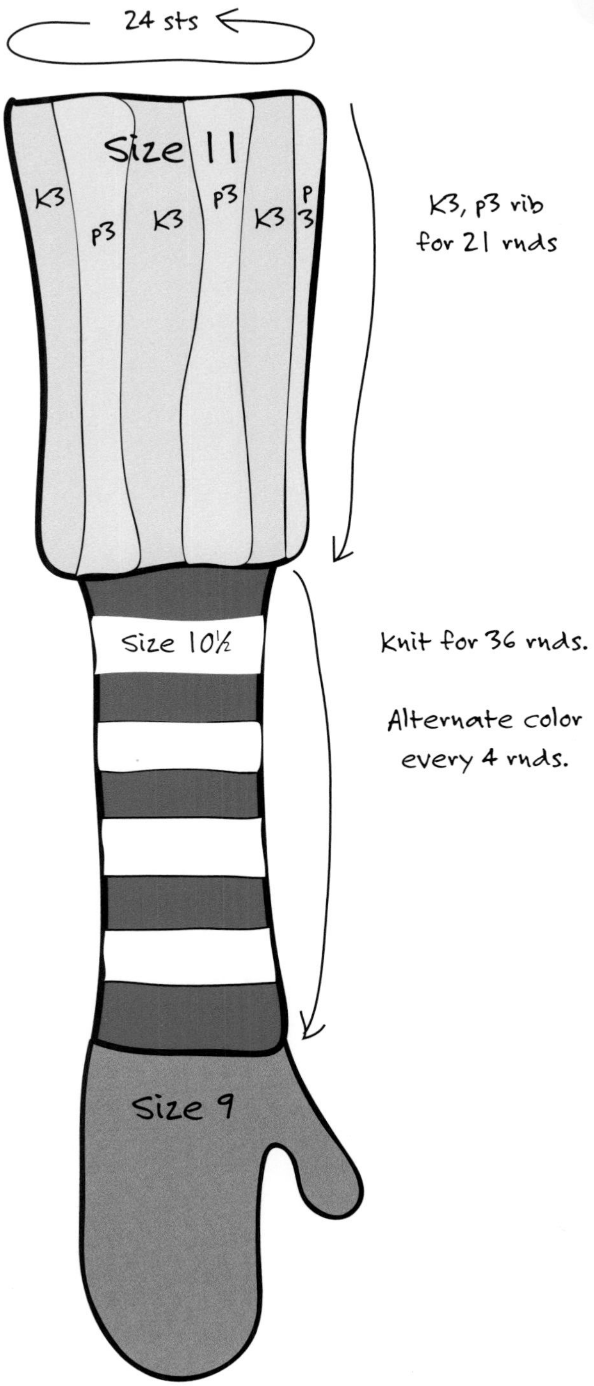
24 sts
Size 11
K3
p3
K3
p3
K3
p3
K3, p3 rib for 21 rnds
Size 10½
Knit for 36 rnds.
Alternate color every 4 rnds.
Size 9

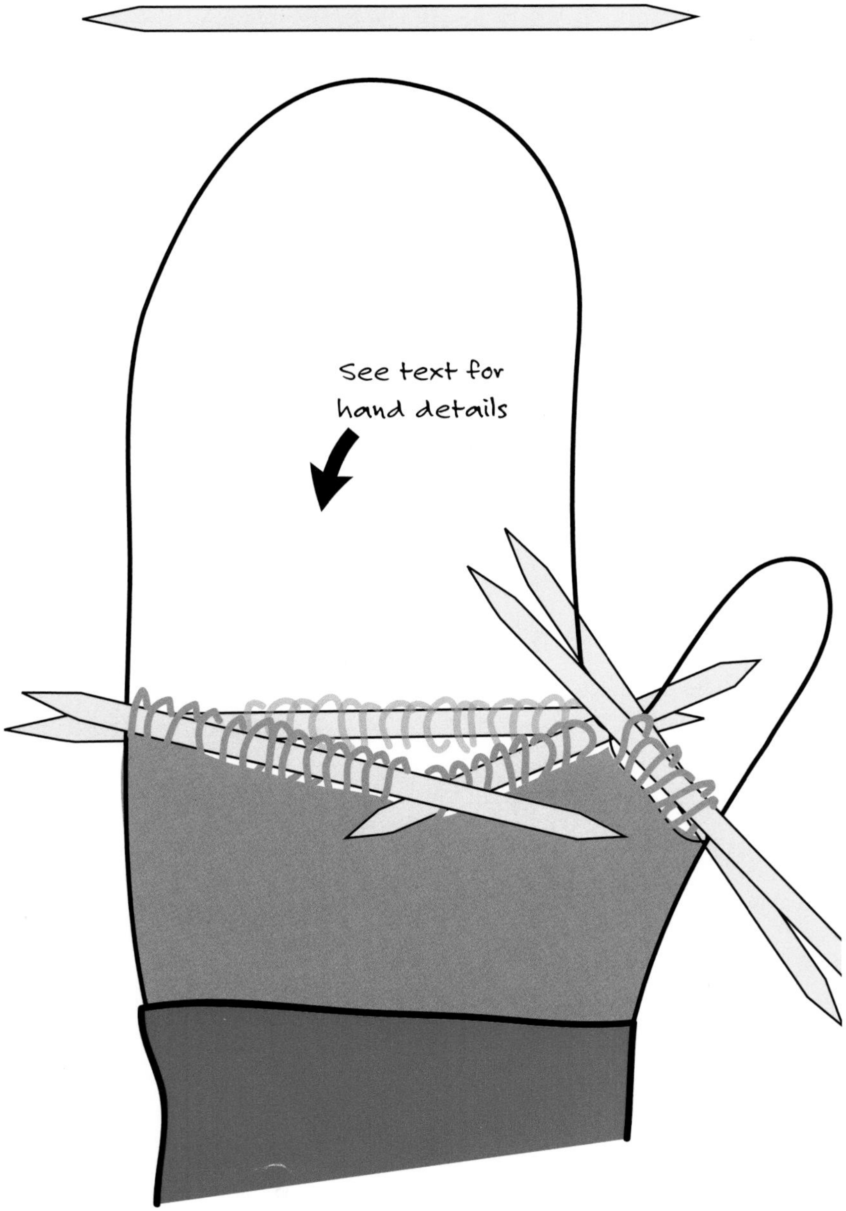
See text for hand details

Thick 'n' thin crazy-carded yarn with nubs in Tencel, linen, cotton, wool, and Sparkle by Drucilla.

Slip Stitch Pixie Hat

This ultra-simple design lets the yarn speak for itself. This is the perfect project to show off extra-textured Nub or Add-In's yarns.

Crochet Skills Required

Chain (ch)
Slip st (sl st)
Single crochet (sc)

Size

Length: 9" (23 cm)
Circumference: 19" (48.5 cm)

Materials

About 4 oz (113 g) thick 'n' thin singles with nubs (see page 86). Reserve 6 strands each 14" (35.5 cm) long
Size I/9 (5.5 mm) crochet hook. Change hook size as necessary to accommodate your yarn and gauge
Tapestry needle

Gauge

11 sc = 4" (10 cm) using size I/9 (5.5 cm)

The Yarn

Simple thick 'n' thin handspun single with nubs

Hat

Crochet a base chain long enough to loosely wrap around wearer's head. Make sure the ch isn't twisted before joining sts into circle with sl st. The RS of work will be facing outward, toward you as you crochet.

Sl st into each ch, working in a continuous spiral. When you reach a nub, pull the nub through the stitch to the front of the work, even if this means making a slightly larger loop. Continue sl st in the next st normally

once you pass the nub. As you circle around and reach the nub again, *do not* crochet through that loop; instead, insert the hook *behind* the nub into the stitch in the rnd below. Essentially, you'll be making a sl st behind the nub.

This will cause the nub to sit up directly on the surface of the crocheted fabric. Sl st the next st in the normal place. When you come around to the nub for the third time, hook into the loop you made *behind* the nub.

Repeat all rnds in this manner until the hat measures about 6" (15 cm) from base ch.

Crown Shaping

Begin decreasing by randomly skipping sts. Random decreasing will give this hat its asymmetry. Continue decreases until the hat measures about 9" (23 cm) or desired length from base ch, and spirals closed. Try the hat on frequently during the decrease rnds to make sure you can achieve the desired length before closing the top of the hat. Fasten off.

Ties

Determine a left and right side of the hat. Using 3 strands of yarn for each side, tie each strand into the hat on the inside with an overhand knot, about 1" (2.5 cm) up from the edge. Tuck the knot end into the work. Working one side at a time, braid the 3 strands together and secure the bottom of the braid with a small piece of yarn, or overhand knot. Ties should be about 10" (25.5 cm) in length when braided.

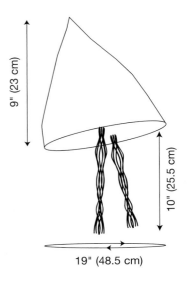

9" (23 cm)

10" (25.5 cm)

19" (48.5 cm)

Finishing

With tapestry needle or crochet hook, weave in ends to WS. Check around the hat, locating all nubs. Make sure each one is pulled out as far as possible on the RS of the hat, so they stand out on the crochet fabric.

Cowgirl Hat

Yarn spun from natural, low-processed plant fibers such as hemp or linen makes an earthy match for this traditional western style hat.

Crochet Skills Required

Chain (ch)
Slip st (sl st)
Single crochet (sc)
Double crochet (dc)

Size

Circumference: 22" (56 cm)
Crown depth: 4" (10 cm)
Brim width: 3" (7.5 cm)

Materials

150 yd (137 m) single-ply wrapped hemp yarn with gold sparkle
Size K/10½ (6.5 mm) crochet hook. Change hook size as necessary to accommodate your yarn and gauge
Tapestry needle

Gauge

12 sc = 4" (10 cm) using size K/10½ (6.5 cm)

The Yarn

Thick 'n' thin single-ply hemp yarn with nubs (see page 86), spun with gold sparkle wrapped (see page 78) in linen thread, by Pluckyfluff

Hat

Foundation ring: Ch 4 and join with sl st to form a circle. Work rnds in a spiral without joining, as follows:

Rnd 1: Work 8 sc into center of ring, place marker. Move marker with each new rnd.

Rnd 2: Cont around without joining, work *1 sc in first sc below, work 2 sc in next sc; rep from * 3 times more to marker—12 sc.

Rnd 3: Work *1 dc in next sc, 2 dc in next sc; rep from * 5 times more to marker—18 sts.

Rnd 4: Work *1 dc in each of next 2 sts, 2 dc in next st; rep from * to marker—24 sts.

Rnd 5: Work *1 sc in each of next 3 sts, 2 sc in next st; rep from * to marker—30 sts.

Cont working 2 rnds dc followed by 1 rnd sc, and working 1 st more between increases until crown fits wearer's head.

Work 1 rnd sc (no increases), then 1 rnd sl st. The sl st rnd is a turning ridge, and the following rnds will form the crown depth.

Now work patt of 1 rnd sc, 2 rnds dc (without any increases), for about 4" (10 cm) from sl st rnd, ending with sc rnd completed.

tip: Check periodically to make sure the crown isn't becoming wavy (too many increases). If this happens, adjust the number of increases made by working more sts between them. If the crown begins to form a point, then there are too few increases, and you'll need to add a few extra. Lay the crown flat on a hard surface; if it lies flat, you have the correct number of increases for your yarn and gauge.

Brim

Work 1 rnd sl st; this will be another turning ridge to help shape the brim. Work 1 more rnd sc; resuming evenly spaced increases as before, work all rnds in dc for about 3" (7.5 cm). Work the final rnd in sl st, decreasing 1 st every 3 sts on each side of brim until 5 decreases are made on each side. The decreases will cause the brim to curl up on the side edges (see

photo below). Make sure you work these sets of decreases exactly opposite each other in order for both sides to be symmetrical. Cut yarn, leaving 4" (10 cm) tail. Fasten off last st, then use crochet hook to weave yarn tail through several sts to secure.

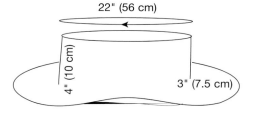

Variation: Cowboy Hat

Work same as cowgirl hat, adding 2 extra rnds to crown depth, and 2 extra rnds to brim width.

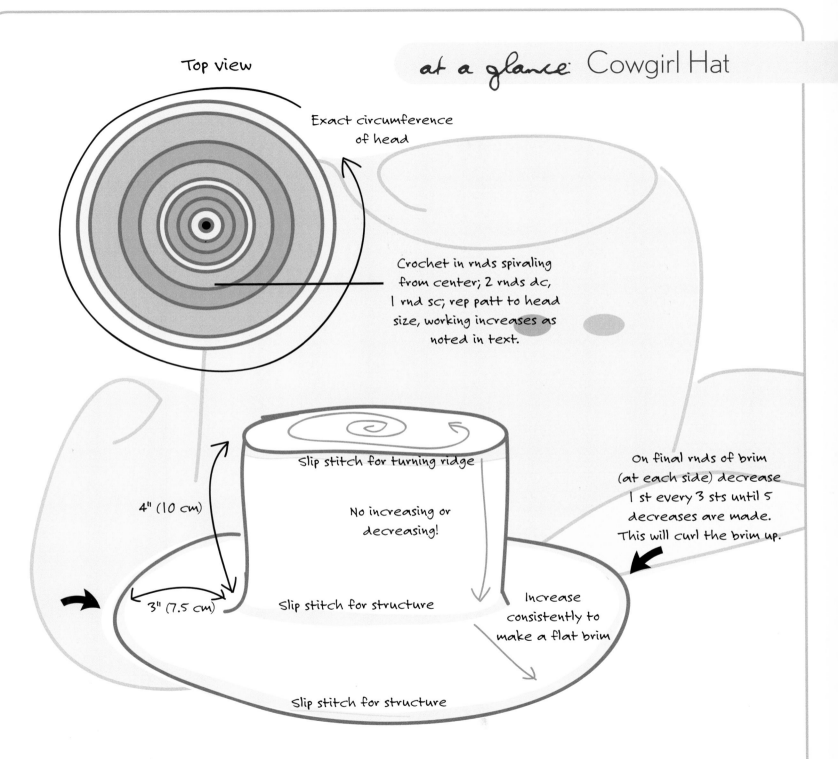

Top view

at a glance Cowgirl Hat

Exact circumference of head

Crochet in rnds spiraling from center; 2 rnds dc, 1 rnd sc; rep patt to head size, working increases as noted in text.

Slip stitch for turning ridge

4" (10 cm)

No increasing or decreasing!

On final rnds of brim (at each side) decrease 1 st every 3 sts until 5 decreases are made. This will curl the brim up.

3" (7.5 cm)

Slip stitch for structure

Increase consistently to make a flat brim

Slip stitch for structure

224

Float Scarf

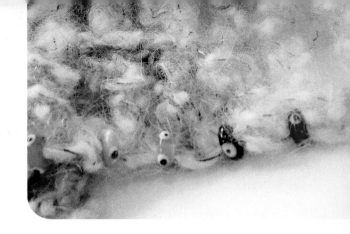

Fluffy handspun mohair makes this scarf virtually weightless.

Crochet Skills Required

Chain (ch)
Triple crochet (tr)
Yarn over (yo)

Size

Length: *60" (152.5 cm)*
Width: *6" (15 cm)*

Materials

120–150 yds (110–137 m) translucent
mohair spun on a pom-pom core thread
(see page 139). Yarn should be thin,
light, airy, and very fuzzy
Size N/15 (10 mm) crochet hook. Change
hook size as necessary to accommodate
your yarn and gauge
Beading crochet hook (hook size depends
on size of bead holes)
20 beads with holes large enough for
2 strands of yarn to pass through
Tapestry needle

Gauge

7 tr = 4" (10 cm) using size N/15
(10 mm) crochet hook

The Yarn

Translucent mohair (see page 138). Mohair and wool core spun with commercial pom-pom plying thread from France.

Scarf

Base chain: Ch 2 very loosely (or use next larger size crochet hook to make larger chains), *remove hook from last ch made, using beading hook, insert hook into one bead and pull the last ch through the bead hole; slide the bead to the left side of the ch it sits on. Insert larger hook back into the ch with bead, ch 1*; rep from * to * 9 times more. You now have 11 ch with 10 beads.

Row 1: Change to size N/15 (10 mm) hook. Ch 3, working into the top loop only of base ch, 1 tr into 4th ch from hook, then 1 tr in each of remaining chs, turn work—11 tr (plus turning ch).

Row 2: Ch 3, 1 tr in top (both loops) of each tr of previous row, turn work—11 tr (plus turning ch). Note: Do not tr in turning ch.

Repeat row 2 until scarf measures about 60" (152.5 cm) or desired length, leaving enough yarn to work one more row, plus 4" (10 cm) to weave in and secure end.

Last row: Ch 3, work 1 tr in top of sts in previous row as follows: **work tr until 2 loops remain on hook, remove larger hook from both loops, place bead on beading hook and insert beading hook into right-most loop, pull loop through bead, remove beading hook; reinsert larger hook back into 2 remaining loops of st, yo and pull through both loops (1 tr made with bead at top); rep from * 9 times more (10 beads), work final tr without inserting bead. Cut yarn and finish off. With tapestry needle, weave in ends to WS, or along side edges. Lightly block to size.

Design and knitting by Jenny Turco, Bee's Knees Knitting, www.beeskneesknitting.com; Blizzard yarn by Pluckyfluff

Softserve Coiled Hat

Graduated coils give this kid-sized hat a sweet lumpy shape.

Knitting Skills Required

Cast on (CO)
Knit (k)
Purl (p)
Backward loop CO (use for increases)
Bind Off (BO)
*Stockinette stitch (ST st): Knit 1 row,
    purl 1 row*

Crochet Skills Required

Slip st (sl st)

Size

Length: 9" (23 cm) including "top knot"
Circumference: 19" (48.5 cm)

Materials

*70–100 yds (64–91.5 m) thick 'n' thin single
    ply yarn in several colors*
*Size 9 (5.5 mm) knitting needles. Change
    needle size as necessary to accommo-
    date your yarn and gauge*
Tapestry needle
Sewing needle and thread
Long sewing pins with large heads
Size J/9 (5.5 mm) crochet hook

Gauge

16 sts = 4" (10 cm) using size 9
(5.5 mm) in St st

The Yarn

Spin a thick 'n' thin single, alternating the colors as you spin. Be sure to
alternate the colors *fairly* evenly.

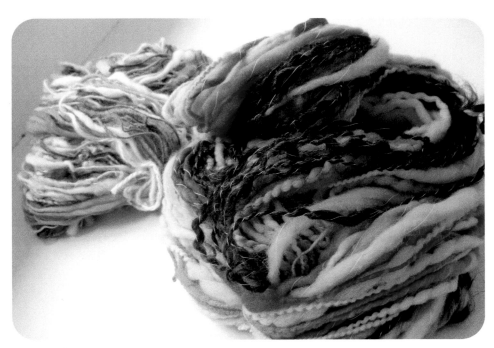

Simple thick 'n' thin handspun single in several colors, by Madeline Tosh,
www.madelinetosh.etsy.com

Hat

CO 1 st.

Row 1 (RS): Using backward loop CO method, CO 1 st, k1—2 sts.

Row 2 (WS): Using backward loop CO method, CO 1 st, p2—3 sts.

Row 3: Using backward loop CO method, CO 1 st, k3—4 sts.

Work even on 4 sts in St st until strip

is long enough to wrap around wearer's head twice. Pinch the strip together at the spot where it fits comfortably on the head; using a threaded sewing needle, pin and then baste the edges together (this forms the lower edge). Cont knitting a few feet (meter) more, coiling the strip around so that one layer sits on top of the previous layer. Stop and baste the coils together about every 3" (7.5 cm) to keep them in place when you try the hat on to determine fit. If the coils need adjusting, remove basting thread, adjust the coils to correct fit, then re-baste. When hat coils cover the crown (about 6–7" [15–18] cm), begin to wrap the coils in smaller and smaller circles to resemble a soft-serve ice cream cone, and form the hat top. Baste the edges together to within the last coil. BO when you have 2–3" (5–7.5 cm) of unpinned knitting. Remove pins.

Using a crochet hook and extra yarn, hook through the BO sts and unpinned side and pull the coil into a

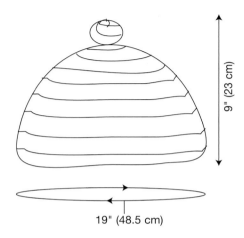

little ball. Tie off the yarn and weave to WS. Turn the hat to WS. Using crochet hook and remaining yarn, beg at base of hat and join the long side edges together using sl st. Cont to sl st around the coils, working upward and as close to the hat top as possible. Leave enough space open to poke the "top knot" through to the RS. Stitch top opening closed with sl st or threaded tapestry needle. Remove basting thread.

Thick 'n' thin wool single spun by Madeline Tosh. www.madelinetosh.etsy.com

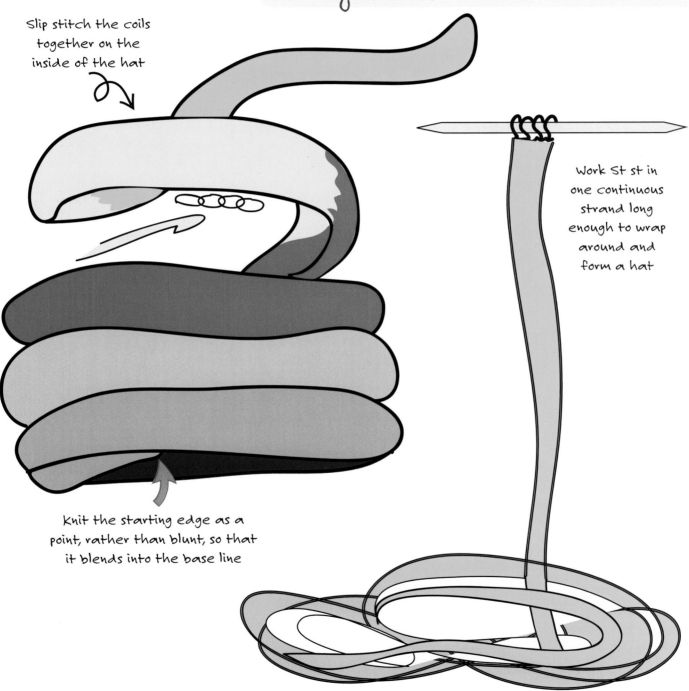

Slip stitch the coils together on the inside of the hat

Work St st in one continuous strand long enough to wrap around and form a hat

Knit the starting edge as a point, rather than blunt, so that it blends into the base line

Truly Hand-Felted Mittens

These hand-felted mittens featuring thick and thin wool yarn spun with tiny vintage hand-crocheted circles. The semi-felted mittens are actually felted on your hand for a perfect fit.

Crochet Skills Required

Chain (ch)
Slip st (sl st)
Single crochet (sc)
Double crochet (dc)
Single crochet decrease (scdec)
Double crochet decrease (dcdec)

Size

Custom, to fit wearer's hands
SIZE SHOWN HERE:
Cuff to finger tip: *10" (25.5 cm)*
Circumference, above thumb:
    9" (23 cm)

Materials

About 5 oz (142 g) fiber or enough to make 80 yd (73 m) thick and thin soft-spun wool yarn with candy-striping and add-ins (see pages 72 and 110) for the mitt hands, and 40 yd (36.5 m) bulky thick and thin for the cuffs (see page 90).
Size K/10½ (6.5 mm) crochet hook for mitts
Size D/3 (3.25 mm) hook for dangle spheres. Change hook size as necessary to accommodate your yarn and gauge

Laundry soap flakes
Large plastic baggie
Rubber band
Tapestry needle
Open-ring stitch markers in different colors
White vinegar

Gauge

7 dc = 4" (10 cm) using size K/10½ (6.5 cm)

The Yarn

Simple thick 'n' thin handspun single in several colors

Soft-spun Targhee wool, candy-striped in weaver's fine-weight wool threaded with vintage hand-crocheted circles

NOTE: These mittens require two types of yarn, one for the cuff (this will *not* be felted) and another for the main part of the mitten. For the cuff yarn, spin a bulky thick and thin single. Make sure this yarn is bulkier than the yarn you spin for the mitt section, as this will ensure that it stands out and really has that fluffy-cuff effect.

For the mitt section soft-spin (see page 70) a thick and thin single and candy-stripe (see page 72) it with a finer yarn or thread for structure, about 8 wpi. The soft-spin will make this yarn much easier to felt, while the striping thread will help hold everything together. Have fun with this project by spinning extra accents into the yarn. Since it will be felted, any non-felting elements will stand out very well. Try vintage needlework, recycled silk, or beads. Our mitts used tiny crocheted circles that were cut from some needlework trim and spun directly into the yarn by threading the striping thread through them. Soak, set, and dry the yarns.

NOTE: You will also need a few yards of smooth singles in two colors, one color for the wrist ties and a contrasting color for the spheres (dangles). You can use handspun or any standard commercial yarn.

These mittens should be crocheted to fit your hands. As you make each mitt, frequently slip your hand inside to make sure the size is right for you. Adjust if necessary by changing the crochet hook size or your crochet tension. The mittens should fit gently

tip: If you crochet loosely, with lots of spaces, the mittens will felt into a thick lace look (pictured). The holes will remain. If you crochet tightly, the fabric will felt into more of a solid material. If crocheting tightly, make sure the mittens fit snugly to begin with, as they will not shrink as much during felting.

and fingers should have plenty of wiggle room. The mittens will shrink to fit snugly during the felting process.

Cuff

Using the bulky cuff yarn, make a chain that fits loosely around your wrist (wrist circumference plus 1/2 to 1" [1.3 to 2.5 cm]). Slip st end sts together to join chain into circle.
Next rnd: Work 1 sl st in each ch.
Next 3 rnds: Cont sl st in each st of previous rnd. If you prefer a longer cuff, work a few more rnds to the desired length (you'll probably need more yarn).
Cut the cuff yarn leaving a 4" (10 cm) tail. Join the soft-spun mitt yarn to beg of rnd.

Mitt

Rnds 1 and 2: Ch 3, work 1 dc in each sl st of previous rnd. Join rnd

with sl st. (These rnds are steps 1 & 2 shown in the At a Glance section, page 235). NOTE: I had to make a couple of dcdec to reduce the circumference after the cuff was completed. Changing to a smaller hook would probably do the same thing.

Slip your hand through the cuff. Looking at the back of your hand, turn the cuff so that the starting point lies on the edge of your hand directly under your thumb. Scoot the work up so that it sits at the base of your thumb. The last stitch in the rnd should be right about where your thumb connects with your hand. Make sure the length is suitable, and not too short. If you need a little more length to cover your wrist adequately, add another dc rnd before beginning the thumb. Remove the mitt and continue.

Thumb

NOTE: It will be helpful to use different stitch marker colors for stitch markers #1 and #2.
Place a stitch marker (#1) into the last stitch in the rnd. Working from the last stitch, ch 4 or 5 sts, or enough chs to go around the thumb

base; join this chain with a sl st to the mitt sts about 3 stitches (place #2 marker here) *before* the last stitch in the rnd (step 3 shown in At a Glance). If necessary, adjust the ch to fit your own hand either by making a shorter or longer chain. You want to create a thumb opening large enough to fit your thumb gently.

Rnds 4 and 5: Ch 3, work 1 dc in the next st and each of the thumb sts, working in the round to form the thumb, join each rnd with sl st into top of ch-3.

When thumb length is about ¼" (6 mm) from the end of your thumb, change to sc.

Next rnd (decreases): Ch 1, scdec around, join rnd with sl st in ch-1 (steps 4–6 shown in At a Glance). Thread yarn tail on tapestry needle and sew thumb top together. Weave in loose end on WS.

Back to the Mitt!

Using the mitt yarn, join with a sl st at the point where you began the thumb chs (dc with #1 stitch marker); insert the hook into both the st with marker and the first ch of the thumb when making the sl st join (step 7 in At a Glance). This will help close any holes at the join, and help the thumb to sit up at the right angle.

Row 4 (step 8): Ch 3, work 1 dc in each st around mitt to marker #2, insert hook into both the st with marker and the last ch of thumb chs to work the last dc. This will help the thumb maintain position and close up any loose spaces. Turn work, and resume working in rnds.

Rnd 5: Ch 3, work 1 dc in next dc and each dc around mitt to marker #1, then work 1 dc in each of the thumb chs (the inside of thumb is facing you), join rnd with sl st to top of ch-3 at marker #2. Remove marker #2. Turn work.

Rnds 6–10: Ch 3, work 1 dc in each dc to end of rnd (marker #1), do not turn at end of rnd, but continue in the same direction for each rnd. When mitt covers the tip of your pinkie finger, begin decreases to gently shape top of mitt. When to begin decreases will depend on the mitt length needed to fit your hand. Try the mitt on after each rnd to determine when to begin decreases.

Rnd 11: Ch 1, change to sc and decrease remaining sts to close the mitt top. Cut yarn and finish off, leaving 4" (10 cm) tail to weave in on WS of work. Remove marker #1.

Repeat instructions for second mitt using your other hand as the guide.

Felt It!

Fill a bucket or sink with about 6" (15 cm) of very hot water (as hot as you can stand without scalding yourself) and ⅛ cup (28 g) of soap flakes. You will felt one mitten at a time *right onto* your hand.

Slip your right hand into a large plastic baggie and wrap it with a rubber band around your wrist to keep it from filling with water. The large plastic baggie will scrunch up and assist with the felting process.

Slip your left hand in the left mitten. Submerge the mitten in the hot soapy water, but do not let the cuff get agitated! (It's okay if the cuff gets wet, but do not felt it.)

Using your right hand, begin vigorously rubbing the mitten with the plastic baggie. This process is just like washing your own hand. Be sure to rub all areas evenly, especially around the thumb and along the edges.

Regularly submerge the mitten to ensure that it stays hot and has plenty of soap.

Continue the felting process for about 20 minutes or until the mitt is felted to a degree that you like.

Rinse all the soap out of the mitten under cold water. Add a small amount (about ¼ cup [60 ml]) white vinegar to the last rinse to remove all the soapiness, and protect the wool.

Gently squeeze out excess water, then place in the washing machine on the spin cycle to remove the remaining water.

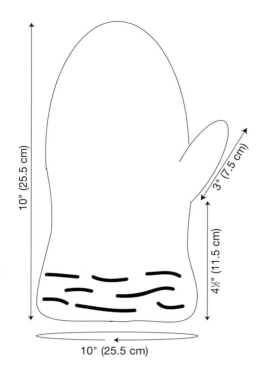

10" (25.5 cm)

10" (25.5 cm)

3" (7.5 cm)

4½" (11.5 cm)

When the spin cycle is finished, remove mitten from the washing machine and put your hand back in. Form the mitten around your hand to a shape that you like. Take your hand out and gently place the mitten in front of a heater to dry.

Repeat the felting process with the second mitten: insert your right hand into the right mitt, and felt it with the large plastic baggie on your left hand.

Dangles!

Use a crochet hook (if there are gaps) or a darning needle (if solid felt) to string a complementary yarn around the wrist above the cuff to act as a wrist tie. Leave both ends of the tie about 8" (20.5 cm) long. Using a different color yarn, knot this second color yarn to one end of the wrist tie yarn, then crochet a small sphere using the second color as follows:
Rnd 1: Leaving a 4" (10 cm tail), ch 3 using the smaller crochet hook, work 4 dc in 3rd ch from hook. Do not join rnd with sl st—simply cont to work around in a spiral.
Rnd 2: Work 2 sc in each st—8 sc.
Rnd 3: Sc in each sc (sphere will be cupped at this point).
Rnd 4: Scdec around 4 sc.
Rnd 5: Scdec 2 times—2 sts. Fasten off leaving 4" (10 cm) tail, thread tail on tapestry needle, and draw through both sts to close sphere. Thread tails on tapestry needle and insert needle into center of sphere, slightly catching a few sts in the inside to secure the ends; withdrawn needle leaving the yarn tails embedded inside sphere. Make another sphere the same for the other end of wrist tie. Repeat process for second mitt.

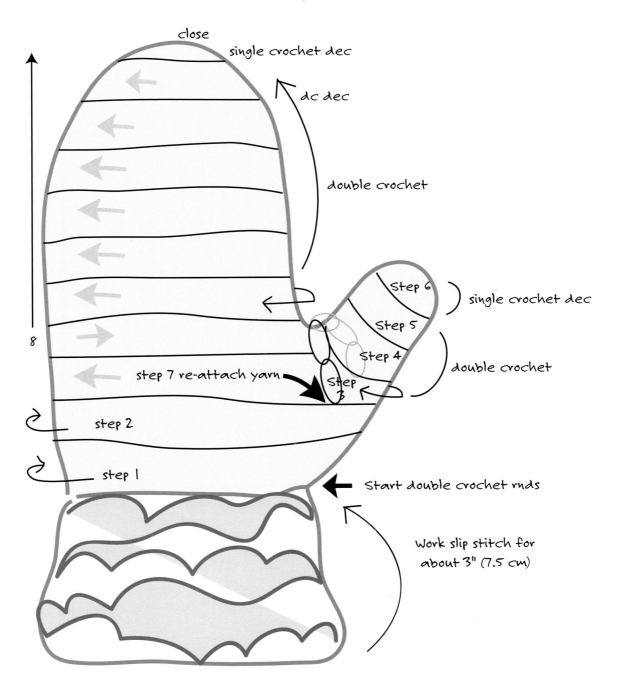

close

single crochet dec

dc dec

double crochet

8

single crochet dec

Step 6

Step 5

Step 4

double crochet

Step 7 re-attach yarn

Step 3

step 2

step 1

Start double crochet rnds

Work slip stitch for
about 3" (7.5 cm)

Felted Shoelaces

Have odds and ends left over from your knitting projects? This project is the perfect use for a few spare yards of your favorite handspun.

Materials

Several yards (m) handspun wool yarn, about 5–6 wpi.

Several yards (m) glittery ribbon or thread

Several yards (m) cotton utility string or waste yarn

Electrical heat-shrinking tubes (available in different sizes at hardware stores; yarn should slip easily into tube before shrinking)

Dishwashing Liquid

Fiber Prep

Spin a wool yarn candy-striped with a glittery ribbon yarn. Optional: For extra dramatic laces, use a jumbo yarn about 4–5 wpi (see page 76).

Felt It!

Arrange the skein in a loop on a flat surface. Using the cotton string (or cotton waste yarn), tie the skein tightly every 3–4" (7.5–10 cm). Fill the washing machine with hot water and a little dishwashing liquid. Drop the skein into the water and run the machine for one full cycle. Fill the machine again and rinse the skein well. Remove the skein. Cut ties off and remove them. Carefully separate each strand of yarn from its surrounding strands. The yarn will be especially felted to itself where it was tied. Once all strands are separated, wind the yarn into a ball.

Shoelaces (Make 2)

Cut a length of felted yarn long enough to lace the shoe you are working with, plus tie a bow. Cut the heat-shrinking tubes into 4 lengths, each about 1" (2.5 cm) long. Thread each end of the yarn through the 1" (2.5 cm) sections of heat-shrinking tube and shrink with a hair dryer. Repeat the process for the second lace. Trim the ends.

tip: For added strength, seal the end of the shoelace with a dollop of hot glue.

Two-ply wool yarn by Jumpsheep, http://jump-sheep.blogspot.com; project contributed by Mirror Mirror; jumbo yarn by Drucilla

Bike (Belt) Bag

Fanny pack? Don't let it happen. This simple belt bag is just the right size for an ID, credit card, house key and lip gloss. What more do you need?

Knitting Skills Required

Cast on (CO)
Knit (k)
Purl (p)
Bind off (BO)
Stockinette stitch (St st): Knit 1 row, purl 1 row

Size

Length: 5" (12.5 cm) with flap closed
Width: 3¾" (9.5 cm) after felting and stitching to leather back

Materials

About 10 – 15 yds (9 – 14 m) 2-ply yarn
Size 9 (5.5 mm) knitting needles. Change needle size as necessary to accommodate your yarn and gauge.
Piece of heavy leather, larger than finished felted piece
Sharp craft knife or scissors to cut leather
Tapestry needle and heavy-duty thread
White vinegar

Gauge

16 sts = 4" (10 cm) using size 9 (5.5 cm) needles in St st.

The Yarn

Simple 2-ply thick 'n' thin handspun yarn, about 12 wpi, by Lynn Wigell

Design and project by Aurora Kross, Brooklyn, NY; Yarn, Autumn Walk, 2-ply wool yarn by Lynn Wigell, www.yarnwench.com

Bike Bag

CO 18 sts. Work in St st for 34 rows. BO all sts. Weave ends to WS.

Felt It!

Fill sink with hot soapy water. Insert knitted fabric into the water, allowing the piece to become completely saturated. Then roll, squeeze, and rub piece around between your hands or across a washing board or hand-held wooden felting board. Dip the piece into the water several times to allow the soapy water to remain in the fibers. After a few minutes the fibers should begin to adhere to each other; if not, keep rubbing and squeezing vigorously until they do. If necessary, dip the piece into cold water, then back into the hot soapy water; repeat as necessary. (The temperature changes will help the felting process.)

Leather Backing

Use the dry felted fabric as your guide by placing it on top of the leather. Mark the leather so that it's slightly wider (about ¼" [6 mm]) on three sides than the knitted piece, but half as long again as the knitted piece to create the flap. I used an edge of the natural hide for the flap so that it would have an interesting shape. I also chose heavy leather so it would be strong and sufficiently weighted to hold the top flap down. I didn't want to add a closure piece. Cut another piece of leather to use as the belt holder. It should be large enough to fit over a belt buckle and pass a belt through, but smaller than the leather purse back.

Sew the belt holder onto the leather back piece. Then sew the back piece to the felt. I chose to sew these two pieces so the seam edges are on the outside (RS). I like the look, and the heavy leather would be too bulky if the seams were sewn on the WS

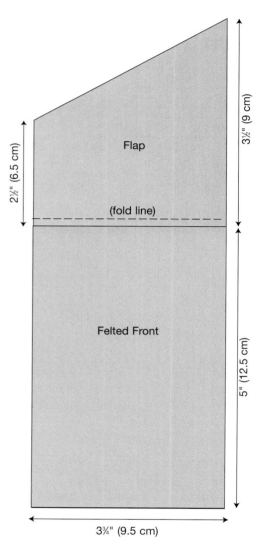

Once the fabric is sufficiently felted, rinse well several times in warm water to remove the suds. You can add about ¼ cup (60 ml) white vinegar to the last rinse water to help remove all traces of soap. Lay the fabric flat and stretch and pat into shape, smoothing out the four sides as evenly as possible. Allow to air-dry completely before attaching to leather back.

and the work turned. Trim the edges of the leather if necessary to match the felt.

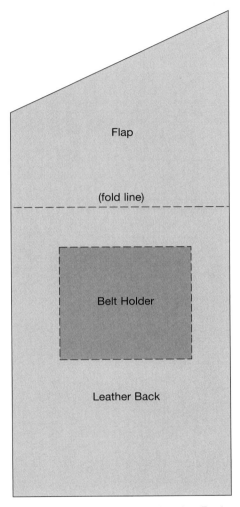

Step 1: Stitch Belt Holder to Leather Back.

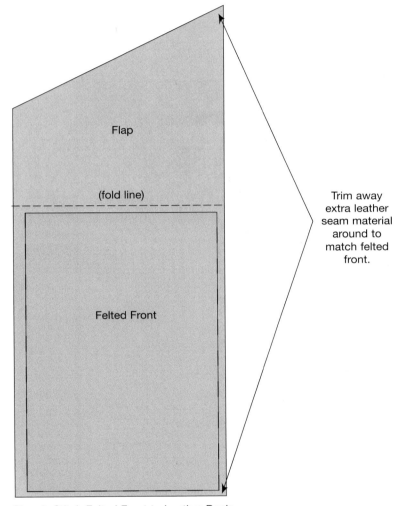

Step 2: Stitch Felted Front to Leather Back.

Spunk Scarf

This is not your grandma's 'possum! You don't even need to know how to knit to make this rural punk scarf. If you're in punk territory you can make this project in the washing machine, and if you're in 'possum country ... well, use a washboard!

Size

Length: 40" (101.5 cm) after felting
Width: 3" (7.5 cm) after felting

Materials

About 45 yds (41 m) mixed selection of handspun punk-style yarns (see chapter 3 for adding extra elements, such as the anarchy patches and pins, when spinning)

About 20 yd (18 m) mohair yarn (commercial is okay)

12–14 prong fasteners, 2¾" (7 cm) long

¼ cup (65g) laundry soap flakes

The Yarn

Punk yarn, wool, plaid fabric, safety pins, and anarchy patches, www.barbesaintjohn.com, by Barbe St John
Corriedale and possum blend spun into a smooth traditional 2-ply yarn, by Lou Andersen, Lofty Lou's, Placerville, CA

Fiber Prep

This is a fast and easy way to make a scarf. Simply cut 20–30 strands of yarn into 65" (165 cm) lengths, or enough to cover a width of 4" (10 cm) when strands are placed side by side. Add to the mix a few strands of extra fluffy lace-weight commercial or handspun mohair yarn. Mohair is excellent for felting, and the long fibers will work as a great binder.

tip: If using a continuous yarn, set your swift to 65" (165 cm) and wind your yarns onto it. Remove the skein and cut through the whole batch. If you don't have a swift, wind the yarns onto a 72" (183 cm) niddy noddy.

Spunk Scarf

Lay yarns out side by side on a flat surface and arrange them to your liking (if you are using different colors, you can control the striping, etc). Once you have them in the order that you want, push the yarns as close together as they will go without overlapping. Starting at one end, gently slip the base piece of the prong fastener underneath the yarns and fold the arms down into place. Slide the fasteners over the arms to secure.

Repeat, placing a fastener across the yarn strands every 3" (7.5 cm) or so. NOTE: Make sure the clips are pushed as far as they will go, and press the fastener together to make sure it clamps the yarn tightly. You can even bend the arms up a little to make sure they don't come apart during felting. If the fastener is too loose, the yarns will slip out or bunch up in the washing machine.

Yarn before felting

Felt It!

Set your washing machine to *hot* and *gentle*, if possible. Put the scarf with

fasteners into the machine. Add the soap flakes. Run through one full cycle. Remove the scarf and check to see if the yarns have adhered to each other; if not, continue agitation by running another full cycle and check the scarf every 5 minutes. If the yarns look too tangled at any point, remove the scarf, straighten the yarns, and reset the fasteners. (There will be *some* unavoidable overlapping and tangling.)

Once the scarf is felted to your liking, set the machine on the spin cycle to remove all excess water. Lay the scarf out on a flat surface and untwist any tangles. Once it is arranged flat and in order, separate the yarns from each other on each far end, creating a short fringe. Remove all fasteners. Use the safety pins in the punk yarn to pin together any areas that appear too loose or misshapen, or attach pins randomly for style.

Lay scarf flat to dry completely.

tip: If there are any loose sections, where the yarns dangle unattractively, tie them together with some extra pieces of yarn, then felt the area by hand.

Preparing the yarn strands for felting

Thrashed Scarves: LIL' THRASHER

Tired of all the hooks and needles? Well, put them away. You are just a string and a washing machine away from the world's coolest scarf.

Size

Length: *36" (91.5 cm)*
Width: *About 3" (7.5 cm), varies depending on number of strands used*

Materials

3–4 oz (84–112 g) wool
3–4 yds (2.75–3.5 m) cotton string
¼ cup (59 ml) laundry soap flakes

Yarn

Bulky merino yarn plied with heart-beaded thread, by Drucilla

Fiber Prep

Spin a bulky thick and thin wool single. Either spin beads into the single (see add-ins, page 110) or you can strand beads onto a plying thread, and ply the entire wool skein (see Thread Plying, page 94).

Felt it!

Lay one skein of handspun out in a loop on a flat, hard surface. Using small sections of cotton string, tie the skein tightly every 4–5" (10–12.5 cm). Using scissors, cut completely through the skein between 2 ties. Place the yarn into the washing machine and wash with soap flakes for one full cycle on hot.

After one cycle, remove the yarn and check to see if it's felted to your liking. If not, put the skein back into the machine for another hot cycle.

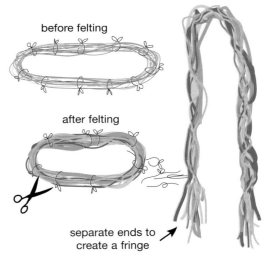

before felting

after felting

separate ends to create a fringe

When the skein is felted, remove the ties and separate the yarn at each end to create a fringe.

NOTE: Use good sharp scissors to trim the scarf of lint or undesirable tangles.

Yarns by Drucilla
Scarf concept and creation by Mirror Mirror

Thrashed Scarves:
WRAPPED AND THRASHED

Skip the knitting and use fabric scraps to wrap and sculpt.

Size

Length: *80" (203 cm)*
Circumference: *About 4" (10 cm), circumference varies depending on number of strands used*

Materials

4–6 oz (113–170 g) wool
3–4 yds (2.75–3.5 m) cotton string
¼ cup (59 ml) laundry soap flakes
4 strips of fabric, each about 2" (5 cm) wide x 16" (40.5 cm) long
Sewing needle and thread to match fabric colors

The Yarn

60–80 yds (55–73 m) handspun wool yarn, any style

Felt it!

Follow the felting instructions for Lil' Thrasher (see page 247) to felt this scarf. After the strands are trimmed and separated, wrap two 6–8" (15–20.5 cm) sections with the fabric strips. Alternate the patterns and colors in the strips for more contrast. Once wrapped to your liking, tuck the ends of the strips into the last wrap and hand-stitch the ends to the wraps to secure. Hand-stitch any sections of the wrap that may loosen and slip.

Yarns by Drucilla
Scarf concept and creation by Mirror Mirror
Top by Aurmour Sans Anguish

Scarf design, traditional yarns, and weaving by Lou Andersen of Lofty Lou's, Placerville, CA; www.knit.us
Nontraditional yarn by Laurence Pocztar
Laine Zin Zin, www.lainezinzin.com

Non 'n' Traditional Woven Scarf

This project is a great example of how traditional and nontraditional handspun yarns can be brought together to make something that is both familiar and surprising. It also illustrates that unusual yarns can be made to work in traditional craft forms such as weaving.

Weaving Skills Required

Idiot's Delight weaving pattern

Size

Length: *50" (127 cm) not including fringe*
Width: *7" (18 cm)*

Materials

*100 yds (91.5 m) traditionally-spun 2-ply
    wool yarn for warp (pictured: white)*
*100 yds (91.5 m) traditionally-spun 2-ply
    wool yarn for weft (pictured: gray)*
*30 yds (27.5 m) non-traditionally spun yarn
    for weft and fringe*

The Yarn

Traditional 2-ply Romney wool yarn
by Lou Anderson; non-traditional
wool/silk/mohair/novelty threads 2-ply yarn
by Laurence Pocztar

Weave!

Lou used the white yarn as warp and the gray and nontraditional yarns as weft.

She set the loom at 8 ends per inch (epi) using a straight twill threading. She then used the Idiot's Delight weaving pattern as follows: one 3 x 1; one 2 x 1; two 4 x 1; three 4 x 1; rep pattern. This gave the fabric a nice textured look.

To start, Lou wove as follows:
1) 4" (10 cm) gray yarn
2) 3" (7.5 cm) nontraditional yarn
3) 4" (10 cm) gray yarn
4) 2 shots nontraditional
    Repeat steps 3 and 4 eight times.
5) 4" (10 cm) gray yarn
6) 3" (7.5 cm) nontraditional yarn
7) 4" (10 cm) gray

Finishing

Remove fabric from loom and lightly full.

Fringe

Cut remaining yarn into strands 23" (58.5 cm) long. Group 4 to 6 lengths together, mixing yarns as evenly as possible for each fringe. Fold strands in half, with crochet hook pull folded edge through short edge, then insert tails through fold and pull tails to tighten fringe. Rep from * 7 times more (8 fringe sections total) across first short edge, then rep 8 fringe groups for second short edge.

KYLE PARKER

Earth Vest

The vest featured in this project is an original design, but any simple vest pattern will suffice. Eliminate all facings and use the main pattern pieces for the woven fabric as well as for the lining pieces.

Weaving Skills Required

Intermediate weaving skills

Size

Chest circumference: 38" (96.5 cm)
Length: 21" (53.5 cm)

Materials

7 skeins nontraditional handspun for weft
400 yd (365.75 m) handspun tweed yarn for warp
Standard commercial vest pattern
1½ yd (1.5 m) cotton fabric for lining
Sewing needle and thread
Rigid heddle loom
Sewing machine
Pins

Vest design, yarn, woven fabric, and images of yarn and fabric by Joan Soth, Camino, California

The Yarn

Types of yarn, clockwise from top left: Candy-striped with slubs. Crazy carded. Uncarded wool. Mohair. Fabric add-ins. Semi-felted wool slubs. Felt add-ins.

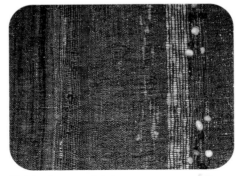

Finished woven fabric

Weave!

String your loom using the tweed yarn for warp. Split each nontraditional yarn skein in half so you will have two repeats of the yarn, one for the front of the vest and one for the back. OPTIONAL: Set aside enough yarn for an additional weaving of the neckband piece and weave this separately. Weave a block of material large enough to fit your pattern pieces. Use a plain tabby weave. This weave structure requires the simplest loom and has the most tie-downs in the weaving. The weave can be accomplished on a simple rigid heddle loom.

The weaving for this project is straightforward; however, it requires some hand manipulating when you come to the more dramatic elements of your nontraditional yarn. To show off these characteristics, simply stop weaving and pull that element or elements to the front of the weaving. This way they will get locked in with the next pass of your shuttle.

Finishing the Fabric

After your fabric is woven, secure the ends by zigzagging them on a sewing machine or serger. Hand-wash your fabric and lay it flat to dry. When the fabric is almost dry, lightly press to block it. This blocking step is important, as the nontraditional yarns in the weft will tend to distort the fabric.

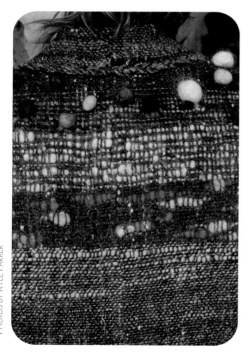

PHOTOS BY KYLE PARKER

Sew the Vest

Cut out the vest pieces from the woven material. Serge or zigzag stitch the edges to prevent fraying. Assemble your vest following the instructions that accompanied the sewing pattern. Cut the lining using the same pieces as the vest. With RS of fabric together, machine stitch the side seams. Press seam open. Pin the lining in place with WS of lining facing WS of fabric. Line the vest right up to the edge. With a threaded

sewing needle, slipstitch the lining into place by hand. This will eliminate much of the bulk that can occur when working with handwoven fabrics.

Additional Detail

Using some of the remaining yarn, make a simple small braid long enough to cover the seam where the neckband attaches to the vest. Leave a small fringe at each end and stitch this over the seam.

15" (38 cm)

2" (5 cm)

9" (23 cm)

21" (53.5 cm)

10" (25.5 cm)

38" (96.5 cm)

Antoinette Skirt

This two-part project features vintage hand-embroidered fabric. The material used here was originally a coverlet for a bed, but the majority of the fabric was stained and worn through. Many parts of the beautiful design and needlework were still in good shape, however, and these parts were carefully cut out and set aside while the remainder of the coverlet was cut into strips and spun into a yarn. The yarn was spun to show off the colorful embroidery threads, and felt beads were added for texture. The yarn and salvaged panels came together to turn a standard straight skirt into a lovely one-of-a-kind creation.

Size
Custom

*Skirt design by Liz Graybeal,
www.ladydandelion.com
Completed skirt by Martha Graybeal,
www.beakandbanana.com
Yarn by Pluckyfluff*

Materials

1½ yd (1.4 m) cotton or linen fabric for skirt

Vintage fabric for inserts (remnants from
    material used for your yarn)

50 yd (45.75 m) handspun yarn spun
    from vintage fabric (see Spinning Fabric,
    page 128)

Standard commercial straight skirt pattern

Sewing machine

Sewing needle and thread

Pins

Zipper, as specified by skirt pattern

Yarn spun from vintage embroidered fabric, wool, and felt beads, by Pluckyfluff

Skirt

Cut skirt fabric as instructed by your skirt pattern. Split all seams 13" (33 cm) up from the hemline and insert triangular-shaped cutouts from vintage embroidered fabric. Triangles should be 13" (33 cm) in length and 9" (23 cm) at the widest edge, with ¼" (6 mm) seam allowances. Sew skirt as directed, inserting triangles into seams, except for the seam with zipper. Leave that seam open so the fabric lies flat and yarn can be easily sewn on.

tip: Leave the bottom of the skirt un-hemmed for a frayed look that will complement the spun-fabric yarn.

Piping

Cut yarn sections into three lengths:
1) Waist to top of triangle (x number of seams).
2) Length of both vertical sides of triangle combined.
3) Entire circumference of hem.

Starting with the vertical seams to the top of the triangles, use a basting stitch to attach the yarn directly along the seam. Once all the vertical seams are attached, sew the yarn piping along the triangle starting at the lower left, traveling up to the point and then returning to the hem on the second vertical edge of the triangle. Repeat this process for all triangles. Last, stitch the yarn along the bottom edge of the skirt. Insert zipper and sew up final seam. Remove basting stitches and any pins that were used during sewing.

Details

If there is any yarn remaining, sew on a looped fringe or a crocheted edge, or cut small 1" (2.5 cm) sections and attach around bottom edge of skirt (as shown here).

at a glance: Antoinette Skirt

Handspun fabric used for piping

Leftover fabric from spinning

Tangled Scarf

Have you ever found skeins in your stash that have begun to unravel, and as soon as you try and put them back together they just get more and more tangled until you finally throw the whole snarled nest down in complete frustration? Well, this project is as easy as that, minus the frustration factor!

Size

Length: *64" (162.5 cm)*

Materials

50 yd (46 m) handspun yarn in skein form

4 or 5 strips of fabric in varying lengths and widths

Handful of lace-weight silk yarn or thread in 24" (61 cm) segments

2-3 lengths of other handspun or novelty yarn for contrast

Blouse by Sapphire Cordial

The Yarn

2-ply handspun recycled denim and organic cotton yarn by Lindsay Nice, Elysium Yarns, http://elysiumyarns.etsy.com

Tangle

Lay your skein out and make sure all strands are loose and free. Lay 2 strips of fabric and one-third of the silk thread on the skein. Grab everything together and just start tangling them! Make sure that you pull the strands through themselves in many different directions to create as many knots as possible, and that the fabric and silk threads are well integrated into the tangles.

Once everything is pretty well clumped together, begin to work the strands into an elongated shape. Evenly distribute the biggest clumps so that the scarf is balanced. Once the strands are stretched out to about 64" (162.5 cm) from one end to the other, and fairly evenly formed, take the strips of fabric and run them through the center of the scarf lengthwise, like a backbone. Tie the ends of the fabric around the scarf to secure, and create anchor points. This will prevent the scarf from becoming unraveled or changing shape. You can also use the novelty yarn as the backbone and use the fabric for strategically placed ties and bows.

Wooldancer Collier

It's all in the twist! A versatile application for super-coil yarn, a collier is essentially a length of active super-coil yarn that is twisted back onto itself, forming a beautiful piece of wearable fiber art. The collier can be worn coiled around the neck or hips or tied around as a head wrap. Once the super-coil yarn has been spun, there are a few steps to take that begin right on the bobbin. The secret of the collier lies in the active twist, so be sure to make it immediately after spinning the super-coil yarn ... if the yarn rests on the bobbin at all, the active twist will be lost and the collier will not coil! All you need to do is try it once, and you'll see just how easy it is to make a collier.

Size
Length: About 3 yds (2.75 m)

Materials
About 2 oz (56.5 g) fiber

Super strong ply thread, such as rayon (do the break test: pull between your hands, if your fingers are red and the thread remains intact, it's probably strong enough!)

Embellishments for the ends of your collier, such as beads, tassels, bells, etc.

Felting needle

Sewing needle and thread

Collier design by Michelle Snowdon, Wooldancer Yarn Designs, www.wooldancer.etsy.com

Spin the Yarn

Spin a thick 'n' thin single yarn with your choice of fiber. Michelle prefers to use super-soft merino for versatility and softness, especially for sensitive necks!

Spin the singles into a continuous super-coil yarn using a super strong ply thread (see super-coil spinning, page 98).

With the bobbin still on the flyer laden with freshly spun super-coil yarn, take the end of the yarn in your hand (Michelle uses her nondominant hand), and slowly wind the yarn around your elbow to hand, as if to make a skein. Wind the entire bobbin

tip: Here's a tip for finishing the end of your super-coil yarn. Take the tip of your singles and spin it back about 90 degrees onto itself (toward the orifice), then bring it down again (toward your body). Repeat this action until the tip of the fiber is firmly spun in. Snip the ply thread, leaving about 12" (30.5 cm) or so extra; you will use this later to attach the embellishments.

in this manner. Take the other end of the yarn in the same hand, so you have both ends held firmly, and *don't let go of them!*

The Coiling Stage

Basically you will fold the yarn in half, thereby letting the active twist join the two halves together. The easiest way to do this is as follows: carefully remove the loops of yarn from your elbow, grip both ends of the yarn in your hand (don't let go!), raise your hand high above your head, and let the rest of the yarn drop toward the floor, allowing the twist to wind its way around, joining the two strands together.

IMPORTANT NOTE: If the yarn drapes on the floor, it will prevent the twist from moving along. Lift the yarn and let it hang … gravity will help the twist to move along into the untwisted areas. If the yarn bunches, tug it down toward the center fold in the yarn. Make sure you don't let go of the two ends!

tip: You may need to help the twist move along the yarn by inching your fingers along, and wrapping the two strands together in the direction of the twist. Doing so will help secure the twist.

Finishing

Join the two ends together with your felting needle. Thread on some felted or wooden beads, a tassel, bells, or whatever takes your fancy. With needle and thread, sew through the embellishments a few times to secure them. Voilá!

Yarn Necklace

It's all about the yarn with this straight-forward design. It's like draping a beautiful skein right around your neck.

Size
Circumference: *42" (106.5 cm)*

Materials
Medley of wool roving, merino top, mohair curls, and strands of fancy threads in assorted colors
Crochet hook, any size
Lingerie bag with zipper

Yarn Necklace
Assemble together all the fibers and yarns listed in the materials section. Pull all the ingredients apart into 3 or 4" (7.5 or 10 cm) pieces and mix them together in a big basket, ready to spin.

Spin!
Using merino combed-top roving, spin 1 yard (.9 m) as an even single (this will be used to tie the necklace together later). Now for the main yarn: pulling random pieces from your basket, spin a thick single with as much twist as possible. Work slowly, adding lots of twist and helping the yarn onto the bobbin by hand, when necessary. Spin through your entire basket of materials.

Form the Necklace
Set your swift circumference at 42" (106.5 cm). Unwind the yarn from the bobbin onto the swift, maintaining tension on the yarn to prevent the twist from escaping. Do not allow the yarn to curl up. Unwind the entire bobbin onto the swift until you reach the merino section. Cut the merino section off the bobbin and hold it in your hand so it does not untwist.

Secure the Yarns
Begin to tightly wrap the merino yarn around the necklace strands for a total of 4" (10 cm); this will anchor all the strands together and prevent them from unwrapping. Insert a crochet hook under the wraps near the trailing end of the merino yarn and pull the loose end through. Loop the end over a few tight strands and discreetly tie off. Tuck the extra length under the wraps.

Set the Twist
Gently soak the necklace in a cold water bath for 10 minutes. Remove and let the water drain off, then place the necklace inside a mesh lingerie bag with a zipper closing. Place the bag in the washing machine on the spin cycle to remove excess water. Remove the necklace from the lingerie bag and place on a towel, forming a little ball. Make sure the necklace stays scrunched up to preserve the twists and coils. Allow to air-dry before moving.

Design and yarns by Laurence Pocztar, Laine Zin Zin, www.lainezinzin.com

Three Way Tie

Handspun yarn is the perfect material to make the typically ordinary men's tie extraordinary. The following are just three ideas, but most handspun yarn styles will work well for a tie project. It is not hard to make an exciting men's tie with nontraditional handspun yarn; the trick is to find a man who is nontraditional enough to wear it!

Tie Project #1, Buffalo Cable Tie

Buffalo down, the "Cashmere of the Plains," makes this classic tie extra soft and rich. Spin a simple thick and thin single-ply yarn, using either buffalo fiber or buffalo down.

Knitting Skills Required

Cast on (CO)

Knit (k)

Purl st (p)

Knit 2 together decrease (k2tog)

Slip slip knit decrease (ssk)

Purl 2 together decrease (p2tog)

Purl 3 together decrease (p3tog)

Cable 4 front (c4f): Slip 2 sts onto cable nee-
    dle and hold in front of the work, k2 sts
    from left needle, k2 from cable needle.

Cable 6 front (c6f): Slip 3 sts onto cable nee-
    dle and hold in front of the work, k3 sts
    from left needle, k3 from cable needle.

Backward loop co

Size

Length: 58" (147 cm)
Width: 3" (7.5 cm) at widest part

Materials

1oz (28 g) Buffalo down, dehaired

Size 9 (5.5 mm) knitting needles. Change
    needle size as necessary to accommo-
    date your yarn and gauge

Recycled silk tie, or lightweight silk fabric
    slightly longer and wider than finished tie

Cable needle

Tapestry needle

Coilless pin

Sewing needle and thread or sewing machine

Iron

Gauge

13½ sts = 4" (10 cm) using size 9 (5.5 mm) knitting needles

Buffalo Fiber compliments of Buffalo Gold, www.buffalogold.net

J. B. SCHUMACHER PHOTOGRAPHY

The Yarn

Simple thick and thin handspun buffalo down single, about 10 wpi

Tie

Cast on 4 sts. Work in Garter st (knit every row) until piece measures about 28" (71 cm).

Next row (RS): K1, increase 1 st using the backward loop CO method, k1, increase 1, k2—6 sts.

Next row (WS): K2, p2, k2.

Next row: Knit all sts. Mark this row with coilless pin as RS of work.

Rep these last 2 rows until work measures about 32" (81.5 cm), ending with WS row completed.

Next row (RS): K4, increase 1, k2—7 sts.

Next row (WS): K2, p2, k3.

Next row (RS): Knit all sts.

Rep these last 2 rows until work meas-

ures 35" (89 cm), ending with WS row completed.

Next row (RS): K5, increase 1, k2—8 sts.

Next row (WS): K2, p3, k3.

Next row (RS): K6, increase 1, k2—9 sts.

Next row (WS): K2, p4, k3.

Next row: Knit.

Rep last 2 rows until work measures about 45" (114.5 cm), ending with RS row completed.

Begin c4f patt as follows:

Rows 1, 3 and 5 (WS): K2, p4, k3.

Row 2 (RS): Knit.

Row 4: K3, c4f, k2.

Row 6: Knit.

Rep these 6 rows 2 times more, increasing 2 sts in the last rep on row 6—11 sts.

Work c6f as follows:

Rows 1, 3, and 5 (WS): K2, p6, k3.

Row 2 (RS): Knit.

Row 4: K3, c6f, k2.

Row 6: Knit.

Rep these 6 rows 3 times more, decreasing 2 sts in the last rep on row 6—9 sts.

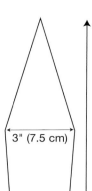

3" (7.5 cm)

58" (147 cm)

1" (2.5 cm)

Shape edge

Row 1(WS): K2, p4, k3.

Row 2 (RS): Ssk, k5, k2tog—7sts.

Row 3: K1, p4, k2.

Row 4: K2, c4f, k1.

Row 5: K2, p2tog, k3—6 sts.

Row 6: K2, k2tog, k2—5 sts.

Row 7: K2, p2tog, k1—4 sts.

Row 8: (K2tog) twice—2 sts.

Row 9: P2tog. Cut yarn and fasten off last st.

Lining

Block knitted tie to desired size, allowing it to dry completely before continuing. Cut the front panel from a silk tie using the knit tie as your pattern, plus ¼" (6 mm) seam allowance all around. Place the silk fabric over the knit tie with WS of silk facing WS of knit tie. Fold the seam allowance to WS, allowing a border of knit material around the silk. Pin silk in place and either hand or machine stitch the lining to the knit fabric. Lightly steam press using press cloth to smooth out any wrinkles.

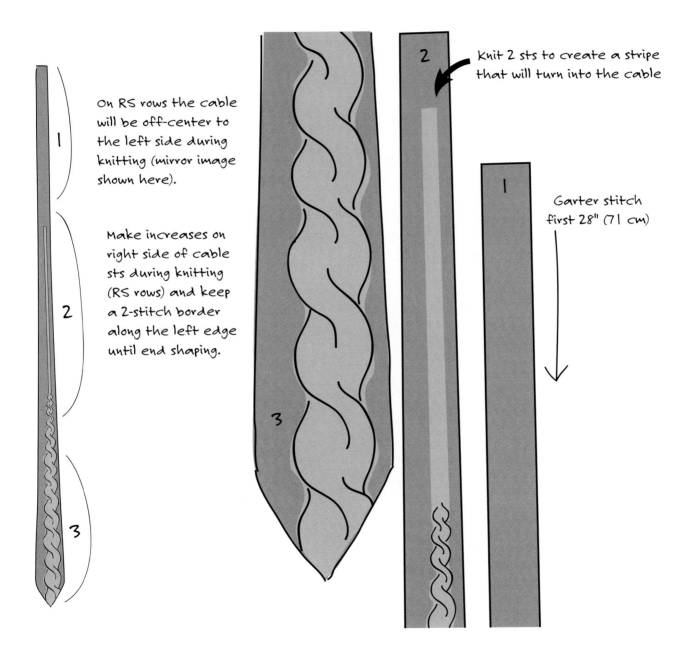

On RS rows the cable will be off-center to the left side during knitting (mirror image shown here).

Make increases on right side of cable sts during knitting (RS rows) and keep a 2-stitch border along the left edge until end shaping.

Knit 2 sts to create a stripe that will turn into the cable

Garter stitch first 28" (71 cm)

Tie Project #2, 2x4 Woven Tie

All you need is a wooden 2x4 and some finish nails to make this loom and weave your tie!

Size

Length: *49" (124.5 cm) not including fringe*
Width: *3" (7.5 cm) at widest end*

Materials

About 80 yd (73 m) handspun yarn for weft (see below for details)

About 160 yd (146 m) fine commercial yarn for warp

Size 9 (5.5 mm) set of double-pointed knitting needles (to use as loom pulls and beater)

Size I/9 (5.5 mm) crochet hook (to pull fringe strands through fabric)

Men's tie to use as template, and optional lining

Tapestry needle

Sewing needle and thread or sewing machine

Wooden 2 x 4

Finish nails 2" (5 cm) long

Double-sided tape

Hammer

Flat metal ruler

Crochet hook, any size

The Yarn

Shown here are sections of the yarn from the beginning and the end of the skein. The yarn on the left was used to weave the narrower two-thirds of the tie, while the yarn on the right was utilized for the wider tie front and the fringe. They are made from the same batt, but one is spun as a tight single and included the short fibers from the small drum after carding (see crazy carding/mini batt, page 65–66) and the other was soft-spun with cocoons (see pages 70 and 86 for spinning instructions).

Fiber Prep

Spin a thick and thin single that progresses from very thin at the beginning of the skein to very *thick and thin* at the end, with many big poofy sections toward the front end. This spinning style will give you more versatility when weaving. Since woven fabrics can be bulky, use the finer yarn for most of the tie that will not show (narrow end to middle of tie) and reserve the more dramatic thick and thin yarn for the front of the tie and fringe.

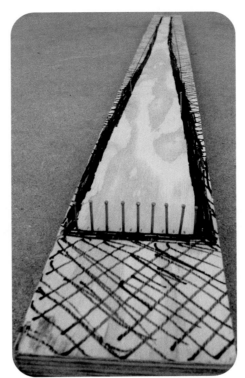

The Loom

You will need a commercial tie to use as your pattern for this project. Select a tie that is the same size and shape that you want to weave. Use a wooden 2x4 (or any flat plank) that is long enough and wide enough to accommodate your tie, with an extra few inches (centimeters) at each end. Using double-sided tape, temporarily stick the backside of the tie to the wood. Use a felt pen and outline the tie, making sure the tie is situated as straight as possible. Remove the tie and any remaining tape.

Using 2" (5 cm) finish nails, hammer a nail into the wood every ¼" (6 mm)

J. B. Schumacher Photography

across the bottom edge of your tie template. You can space the nails further apart if you use a bulkier yarn for the warp, but then you'll have a bulky, thick tie. Next, move up to the top of the plank (this will be the narrow end of the tie template) and hammer the nails across every ¼" (6 mm).

Warp

Choose a yarn for the warp that is more delicate than your handspun, yet is strong. For this tie I chose a silk lace-weight yarn and blue linen with sparkles. Measure the length of the tie pattern and add 6" (15 cm) for fringe (more if you want a longer fringe, less if you plan to use a shorter fringe). Set your swift to this measurement.

Calculate the number of strands you need by counting the number of nails at the bottom of the template (wide end of tie) and multiply that number by a minimum of 3. If you are using a bulky warp yarn you will only tie 3 strands on each nail. If you are using very delicate, fine threads/yarns you may want more (4–5 strands per nail are shown in the photo).

Once you know the number of strands needed, attach the warp yarn/thread to the swift and begin winding. Each rotation of the swift will give you one strand for the warp. Complete the total number of rotations needed for all the strands. Using scissors, cut through the entire group; this should leave you with even strands.

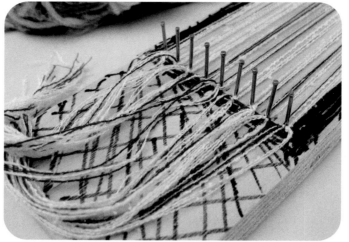

Lay them out in a flat and untangled line by the loom. Separate the strands into groups to be tied on each individual nail (for example, if you use 4 strands per nail, separate them into groups of 4).

String the loom

Grab a group of strands and make an overhand knot about 2" (5 cm) from the end. This knot will go over the nail at the narrow end of the template. Place the knot over the nail so that half the number of strands are on one side of the nail, and the other half are on the other side. Pull the strands down flat and even to the other end of the loom (make sure not to cross them!) Tie them together in a square knot around the first nail at the base of the loom. Make sure you pull these strands nice and tight as you make the knot. There should be 5–6"

(12.5—15 cm) of fringe extending from the bottom of the loom (this will become part of the tie fringe). Repeat until all nails are strung.

Pulls

Using some of the delicate yarn or string and a double-pointed knitting needle (dpn), make the pulls to lift the alternating strands up (this will make the weaving go much faster!).

If you have 10 nails, there will be 20 alternating strands. On the first dpn needle, loop around the even-numbered strands, and on the second dpn loop around the odd-numbered strands. Make each loop even across the needle and tie it off tightly.

Loop the string around every other strand or group of strands.

Weave!

Starting with the dramatic thick and thin end of your skein, cut a few yards (meters) from the main ball and wrap around a flat metal ruler (the ruler will be your bobbin). *Lift up on the first pull (dpn) and slide the ruler/yarn through the space provided. Turn the ruler around, lift up the second pull, and slide the ruler/yarn through that space. Repeat from *. Use an extra dpn to tamp down the weaving as you go, making sure the weaving yarn lies as close together as you want it.

Weave from the bottom up, changing to thinner and thinner yarn as you go.

As you near the end you will have to remove the pulls and weave the last couple of inches (centimeters) with a threaded tapestry needle. Cut the yarn, leaving about 6" (15 cm) tail. Using the tapestry needle, thread the yarn tail neatly to the WS of the work and secure. Secure the yarn the same way at the other end of tie.

Fringe

Cut a few 12" (30.5 cm) lengths of handspun yarn (use as many lengths as will look good with the yarn you're working with). Fold each length in half; * working one strand at a time, loop the fold through the bottom edge (wide end) with a crochet hook. Grab the loose tails and insert them through the fold, then pull the tails to tighten the fringe. Repeat from *, spacing each strand evenly across the wide end. (I used only 5–6 strands and mixed the bulkier yarn with the fine commercial weft yarn for a more organic appearance.)

Line It! (optional)

For an added touch, cut the front panel from the tie you used as a template. Attach the WS of the lining to the WS of the fabric, following lining instructions for Tie #1, Buffalo tie.

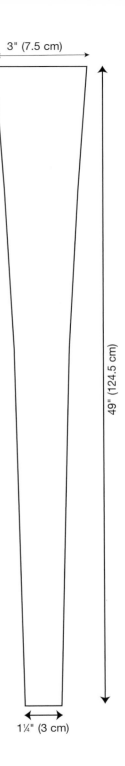

3" (7.5 cm)

49" (124.5 cm)

1¼" (3 cm)

Tie Project #3, Semi-Felted Bubble Tie

Handspun wool, semi-felted mohair yarn by Linda Scharf, www.stoneleafmoon.com

Crochet Skills Required

Chain (ch)

Single crochet (sc)

Double crochet (dc)

DC2tog (dc decrease): Yo, draw up loop in next st (3 loops on hook); yo, draw hook through first 2 loops on hook (2 loops on hook); yo, draw up loop in the next st (4 loops on hook); yo, draw hook through first 2 loops (3 loops on hook), yo, draw hook through all 3 loops—1 dc decreased.

Size

Length: *56" (142 cm) not including fringe*
Width: *4" (10 cm) at widest end*

Materials

About 85 yd (78 m) handspun singles with mohair bubbles (see Semi-Felted Bubbles, page 114)

Size J/10 (6 mm) crochet hook

Men's tie to use as template

Tapestry needle

Gauge

13½ sts = 4" (10 cm) using size 9 (5.5 mm) needles in St st

The Yarn

Simple thick and thin merino handspun single, with semi-felted mohair bubbles spun in, about 10 wpi

Fiber Prep

Spin a fairly smooth single for about one-third of the yarn, then begin adding the mohair bubbles in smaller bits, increasing their size during the last one-third of the yarn. The larger mohair bubbles should be worked on the front section of the tie only; they are too large and bulky if crocheted on the back section or under the shirt collar. For added texture, spin in novelty yarn scraps (pictured: linen yarn dangles around the mohair bubbles).

Working at the widest end of the tie, ch 10 sts.

Tie

Row 1: Dc into 4th ch from hook, 1 dc in each ch to end—8 dc (includes ch 3), turn work.

Row 2: Ch 3, dc2tog, dc to last dc, work 2 dc in last st, turn work.

Row 3: Ch 3, dc across to end, turn work.

Rep rows 2 and 3 for patt. Pull all semi-felted bubbles to the front of

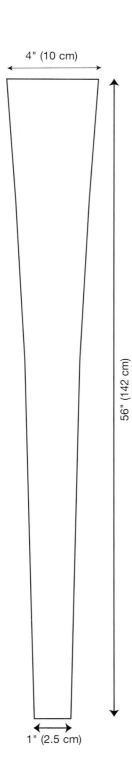

4" (10 cm)

56" (142 cm)

1" (2.5 cm)

the work with the crochet hook or your fingers. Using the commercial tie as a reference; lay the work against the tie periodically to determine when to decrease an extra st in order to shape tie.

When tie is finished, lightly block, taking care not the flatten the bubbles.

NOTE: Some bubbles may be too large to manipulate as dc; when that happens, work them as sc. If any large bubbles fall under the shirt collar, remove them with scissors, taking care not to cut the main yarn.

The Yarn Gallery

chapter 7

All yarns by *pluckyfluff* except as noted.

Trumpet Vine
Thick and thin wool, mohair, sparkle single ply in foggy rainbow colors. Throughout are vintage beads nestled in green sparkle mohair poofs

Little Prairie Massacre

Bulky single in natural white Icelandic wool, hand-dyed fibers, silk waste, fabric, flowers, rubber cherries, and a 1940s vintage doll with open/close eyes, leather and hide doll chaps, and floral doll shirt. The length of the yarn is spun with a delicate pale pink bubbly thread and coral pink silk thread

Hand-dyed rainbow wool and electric blue shimmer spun on an elastic-thread core

Alien Incubator
Single-ply wool with semi-felted wool bubbles

Santa Smoothie
Self-striping wool yarn with uncarded white Lincoln locks

Earthsea
Thick 'n' thin blue merino single with multicolored uncarded Lincoln locks and gold sparkle, by Drucilla

Spacegirl

Self-striping yarn in orange, pink, and white wool with whole sections in solid sparkle. Tangles in metallic thread throughout, and the entire length of yarn is wrapped with a spacey gray nylon ribbon

Cat Hairball

Single-ply yarn in coarse Lincoln wool and Persian cat hair. Soft yet scratchy!

The Emperor Has No Clothes

Bulky single spun from reclaimed vintage embroidered muumuu. Spun with wool, threads, and sparkle/felt bobbles

Magic Worm

Delicate two-ply yarn rainbow wool, blue mohair, and super-coiled green silk

Victoria

Coily spun two-ply yarn in hand-dyed flesh pink merino with recycled silk rosettes

Swansong
Quill-spun bulky yarn in wool, sequins, fabric, and white feathered swans

Firebubble

Wool and sparkle pom-poms,
by Elizabeth O'Donnell

Christmas Turkey

Wiggly two-ply in brown corridale
with green chenille, blue tinsel, and
red/white sparkle thread

Burger Bar

Two-ply multicolored wool yarn, by Claire X, www.missbell.co.uk

Soft-spun hand-dyed thick 'n' thin single-ply wool/mohair yarn, by Ozark Handspun

Think Love, Live Joy
Material Whirled Luxurious
silk/novelty thread single ply,
by Angela Place

Thick 'n' thin single-ply
wool yarn spun from mis-
cellaneous fibers gleaned
from the small drum after
carding, by Aisha Celia
Designs (see Mini Batts,
page 66)

Screamer

Triple plied alpaca with novelty
yarn and sequins, by Yarn Punk

Punked

Wool/alpaca pun with skulls,
pins, yarn scraps, and charms,
by Yarn Punk

Wildflowers
Chunky single ply hand-dyed yarn spun from uncarded wool, by Fuzzy Fibers

Single-ply wool yarn spun with hand-felted vegetables and hand-sewn lettuce leaves, by Liz Graybeal

Collection of three hand-spun yarns by Laurence Pocztar, Laine Zin Zin

Bulky thick 'n' thin single-ply wool yarn spun on a drop-spindle, by Sandy Ryan, Homestead Wool and Gift Farm

Two-ply wool yarn spun with heart beads,
by Daniela Kloppmann, Felt Studio

Single-ply wool yarn
with bells, by Tove
Skolseg, Norway

Sweet Samsar

A Merino yarn plied with pom-pom thread, by Mallory Jankowski

Two-ply wool yarn in ocean blues, by Miss Hawklet

Before and After

Before:

I Am Not the Bot You're Looking For
Steel wool (fine, medium, and coarse grade) spun with scouring pad curls, sink chains, and springs

After:

The Ultimate Clubbing Bag
Steel wool yarn, stainless steel chain, and carabiner

Before:

Cozmic Debris

Wool, wire, tangled metallic threads, and sparkle

After:

Crocheted hat with reclaimed denim accent, by Shannon Herrick, www.thespunmonkey.com

KYLE PARKER

Before:

Cuddle Bug

Natural gray wool spun with rainbow wool sparkle cocoons

After:

Handknit cape, by Jennifer Faye Walchli Lowman

Resources

Fiber Suppliers and Farms

Buffalo Gold

www.buffalogold.net

American bison down and roving, as well as yarn, leather, knit kits, buffalo felt, and buffalo buttons

P.O. Box 516 / 11316 CR 604

Burleson, TX 76097

817-992-8220

Ebay

http://crafts.listings.ebay.com; scroll down to spinning section

Roving, wool, fibers, spindles, spinning wheels, and other spinning items

Jungle

www..jungle.etsy.com

Jungle felt sushi rolls from Felt Add-Ins, page 110

Homestead Wool and Gift Farm

www.homesteadwoolandgiftfarm.com

Animal-friendly farm providing an assortment of fibers, wool, and hand-spun yarn

Monroe, WI

608-966-3943

Wynham Farms

www.gotmygoat.com

Mohair, blends, fibers, and mohair clouds (see Translucent Mohair, page 138)

Brighton, CO

303-857-4095

Contributors

Patterns/projects

Aurora Kross

Design and pattern, *Bike Bag*, page 238

Brooklyn, NY

Cindy S. Cafaro

Knitting, *Twizzler Scarf*, page 178

www.flickr.com/photos/glccafar

Deborah Dant

Snuggle Shrug, page 194

Tesque, NM

Joan Andrews Soth

Yarn, weaving, sewing, and design, *Earth Vest*, page 252

Distinctive Creations

Camino, CA

Kate Bürge and Rachel Price

Yarn and patterns, *Spincycle Poncho*, page 204 and *Spincycle Third Wave Harf*, page 200

Spincycle Yarns

www.spincycleyarns.com

Laurence Pocztar, France

Yarn Necklace, page 266

Laine Zin Zin

www.lainezinzin.com

lainezinzin@club-internet.fr

Liz Graybeal

Skirt design and concept, *Antoinette Skirt*, page 256

www.ladydandelion.com

Lou Andersen

Yarn and pattern, *Non 'n' Traditional Woven Scarf*, page 250

Lofty Lou's

585 Main St.

Placerville, CA 95667

530-642-2270

www.knit.us

Martha Graybeal

Sewing and construction, *Antoinette Skirt*, page 256

www.beakandbanana.com

Madeline Tosh
www.madelinetosh.com
www.madelinetosh.etsy.com
Yarn from *Softserve Coiled Hat*, page 226

Mallory Jankowski
www.plinthesky.com
Gallery, page 295

Material Whirled
Angela Place, Reenie Hanlin
www.materialwhirled.com
Gallery, page 289

Miss Hawklet
www.misshawklet.com
Gallery, page 296

Ozark Handspun
www.ozarkhandspun.com
Gallery, page 288

Rachael-Marie
www.knittydirtygirl.com
Yarn "Natural" from *Secret Stripe Gauntlet Mitts*, page 210

Sandy Ryan
Homestead Wool and Gift Farm
www.homesteadwoolandgiftfarm.com
Gallery, page 293

Tove Skolseg
Lillehammer, Norway
www.skolseg.no
Gallery, page 294

Yarn Punk
www.yarnpunk.etsy.com
Gallery, page 290

Photography

Kyle Parker
Placerville, CA
Shoshin Images
www.shoshinimages.com

Pierce Schmidt Photography
Chicago, IL
pierce@pierceschmidt.com

Jen Schumacher
J.B. Schumacher Photography
jbsphoto@gmail.com
Three Way Tie, page 268

All photography by *pluckyfluff*
unless otherwise noted.

Styling & Hair

Amy Fox
Bella Capelli Salon
580 Main St
Placerville, CA 95667
(530) 344-0320
Three Way Tie, page 268

Clothing

Jamaica Cole
Sapphire Cordial
www.sapphirecordial.com
Clothes modeled for *Tangled Scarf*, page 260

Tawny Holt and Julie Edwards
Armour sans Anguish, clothing and accessories made from 100 percent recycled materials
http://www.armoursansanguish.com
Clothes modeled for *Pretty 'n' Punk Neck Cuff*, page 170; *Everything Nice Pill Box Hat*, page 40, and *Wrapped and Thrashed*, page 248

Acknowledgments

This book is truly a collaboration of crafters, spinners, artists, family, and friends. It could not have happened without everyone's contributions, input, and support. Thank you to all of the spinners who graciously donated their beautiful yarns. Thanks to the crafters who skillfully created projects and shared their patterns. A special thanks to the animals at Homestead Wool and Gift Farm for their wonderful fibery contributions. Massive thanks to Jenny and Aurora for saving my butt. Thanks to all of my drop-dead-gorgeous models: Hannah, Corrie, Britanny, Anna, Rita, Christy, Katelyn, April, Jennifer, Kyle, Gavin, Fayth, Layla, Julie, Sara, Tara, Joel, Dan, Pixel, Scarlett, Erin, Eva, and Casey. Thanks to Jennifer for shooting the guys in ties. Kyle, can't even be thanked enough, for putting up with me and delivering the most stunning photographs ever.

Thank you to the amazing clothing designers whose work gave this book some style: Tawny Holt and Julie Edwards (Armour sans Anguish) and Jamaica Cole (Sapphire Cordial). Special thanks to Lou and the amazing staff at Lofty Lou's for all of the advice, encouragement, and on-the-spot knitting lessons! Thanks to Mary Ann Hall and Jean Lampe for tolerating my disorganization and polishing my rough effort into a high shine. Thank you to my mommy, the best mommy ever, for all the support in all of its forms. And thanks, most of all, to my husband Joel (aka Drucilla … aka Mirror Mirror), for the yarn, for the creative projects, for the support, for picking up my slack, and for the love. Thanks.

Thanks to all of you who drop in on the site and blog, for your interest and e-mails—I appreciate every single one. Thanks for keeping the world spinning!